Henry Hutchinson Montgomery

The Light of Melanesia

Henry Hutchinson Montgomery

The Light of Melanesia

ISBN/EAN: 9783337253950

Printed in Europe, USA, Canada, Australia, Japan

Cover: Foto ©ninafisch / pixelio.de

More available books at **www.hansebooks.com**

THE LIGHT OF MELANESIA.

A RECORD OF THIRTY-FIVE YEARS' MISSION WORK IN THE SOUTH SEAS;

WRITTEN AFTER A PERSONAL VISITATION MADE BY REQUEST OF THE RIGHT REV. JOHN SELWYN, D.D., LATE BISHOP OF MELANESIA.

BY

H. H. MONTGOMERY, D.D.,

BISHOP OF TASMANIA.

PUBLISHED UNDER THE DIRECTION OF THE TRACT COMMITTEE.

LONDON:
SOCIETY FOR PROMOTING CHRISTIAN KNOWLEDGE,
NORTHUMBERLAND AVENUE, W.C.;
43, QUEEN VICTORIA STREET, E.C.
BRIGHTON: 129, NORTH STREET.
NEW YORK: E. & J. B. YOUNG AND CO.
1896.

DEDICATED

TO

BISHOP JOHN SELWYN,

THE NOBLE SON OF A NOBLE FATHER,

WHOSE NAME, WITH ITS DOUBLE MEMORY,

LINKED WITH THAT OF PATTESON,

SAINT AND MARTYR,

WILL LIVE FOR EVER IN THE SOUTH SEAS,

AND WHEREVER THE ANGLICAN CHURCH IS KNOWN,

ENROLLED AMONG THE GREAT MISSIONARIES

OF THE CATHOLIC CHURCH.

PREFACE.

THIS book has appeared already in the form of articles in the Tasmanian *Church News* during 1893-4, and they are now given to the public through the generosity of the S.P.C.K., in the hope that they may draw greater attention to the work of one of the noblest missions of our day. During the illness of Bishop John Selwyn I was called to do what I could for the Mission, starting on my tour from Auckland in August, 1892. The Mission ship was my virtual home from that date until the 21st of October, when I was dropped at Vila in the New Hebrides, to find my way back to Sydney, and thence to Tasmania. During these months I spent a week at Norfolk Island, and afterwards I landed on almost every island in charge of the Mission in the New Hebrides, Banks, Torres, Santa Cruz, and Solomon groups. It was, on the whole, the most wonderful experience of my life, for I had to face problems of humanity quite new to myself, and did so in the company of men of great experience, who love the black races. I did not attempt to learn the languages spoken in these islands; I considered that in my case it would have been time wasted. But I spent every available hour in making myself acquainted with the history of the Mission, and I obtained access to every report and "Island Voyage" and published book from 1857 up to the present time. These I analyzed carefully, and submitted the result of my labours to the clergy of the Mission for correction and amplification, adding of course conclusions drawn from my own observation. I cannot, indeed, claim that there is much original matter in these pages, but I venture to hope that the method I have adopted may assist clergymen and those who wish to lecture on the Mission. I have taken each island in turn by itself, and have striven to give its history as a mission centre from the earliest days up to the present day. I trust that the publication of the "Melanesian Prayer Cycle" may lead many to desire a fuller knowledge of each centre, and this information I have striven to give. A visitor has one advantage over the veteran missionary in the field. He views everything as new and interesting, and if he can only be accurate he ought to be able to impart some of his enthusiasm to his readers. I have owed Bishop John Selwyn a debt of gratitude for the last twenty years as revealing to me the beau ideal of a missionary. But he has added this above all, that by his invitation to assist him he has linked me for life with his great mission, and if some day I could give a son to the work, it would be a cause for thankfulness thus to be able to be drawn still closer to regions with which the names of Selwyn and of Patteson are inseparably connected. There is a dark side to the story of the coming of the white man into the South Seas. But no one can doubt the truth of the late Dr. Guppy's words in alluding to the Mission in his book on the Solomons: "The work of the Melanesian Mission has been the only redeeming feature in the intercourse of the white man with these islanders."

The illustrations are from photographs taken chiefly by Dr. Welchman and the Rev. A. H. Brittain during my tour; a few are my own handiwork. The apparatus belonged to Mr. Beattie, photographer, Hobart, by whose directions we were able to save some ten dozen views from injury until he could develop them. Mr. Beattie is ready to supply photographs and lantern slides at moderate cost. The photograph of Taki is given by the kind permission of Captain Davis, R.N. For the index and for supervision of proofs in England I am indebted to the kindness of the Rev. A. V. Magee.

BISHOPSCOURT, HOBART,
    January, 1896.

CONTENTS.

CHAPTER		PAGE
I.	Early Days of the Melanesian Mission ...	1
II.	Norfolk Island	11
III.	The Norfolk Islanders—their Customs and Language	22
IV.	Life on Board the "Southern Cross"	28
V.	The Banks Islands—Mota	44
VI.	Santa Maria, Merelava, Merig (Banks Islands)	58
VII.	Vanua Lava, Ureparapara (Banks Islands)	74
VIII.	The Religion of the Melanesians ...	88
IX.	Motalava, Ra, Rowa (Banks Islands) ...	95
X.	The Torres Group—Toga, Lo, Tegua, Hiw	103
XI.	Suqe—Charming	115
XII.	The Santa Cruz Group	123
XIII.	Nelua, Santa Cruz—Te Motu	133
XIV.	Taape, Carlisle Bay, Reef Islands, Nukapu, Pileni	143
XV.	The Solomon Islands, San Cristoval ...	160
XVI.	Maleita (Solomons)	175

CONTENTS.

CHAPTER		PAGE
XVII.	Guadalcanar, Ulaua (Solomons) ...	189
XVIII.	Florida (Solomons) ...	203
XIX.	Florida (*continued*) ...	211
XX.	Ysabel, New Georgia (Solomons) ...	221
XXI.	The New Hebrides—Raga, Opa, Maewo ...	234
Appendix I.—Tabular Statement ...		247
,,	II.—The Labour Traffic ...	249
,,	III.—Problems of the Future ...	251

LIST OF ILLUSTRATIONS.

	TO FACE PAGE
BISHOP JOHN SELWYN	*Frontispiece*
REV. CECIL WILSON	1
INTERIOR OF ST. BARNABAS (NORFOLK ISLAND)	13
CRICKETERS AT ST. BARNABAS (NORFOLK ISLAND)	16
CAPTAIN BONGARD OF THE "SOUTHERN CROSS"	28
ARCHDEACON PALMER AT MERELAVA	66
CHILDREN AT RA (BANKS ISLAND)	95
THE "SOUTHERN CROSS" OFF SANTA CRUZ	123
MR. FORREST AT NELUA, AND FEATHER MONEY	133
COMMODORE GOODENOUGH'S CROSS, SANTA CRUZ	146
BISHOP PATTESON	150
BISHOP PATTESON'S CROSS, NUKAPU	158
CHURCH AT HONGGO (FLORIDA)	205
PARLIAMENT AT HONGGO (FLORIDA)	215
A CHIEF OF OPA (NEW HEBRIDES)	238

Rev. Cecil Wilson.

THE LIGHT OF MELANESIA.

CHAPTER I.

EARLY DAYS OF THE MELANESIAN MISSION.

IN the end of 1847, Bishop Selwyn (the elder) made his first journeys into Melanesia. In 1866 the settlement at Norfolk Island was formed under the supervision of the Rev. J. Palmer, who is still with the Mission. The area of the field of work, extends from a portion of the New Hebrides to the Solomon Islands. Formerly it included the Loyalty Islands, but these were surrendered to the London Missionary Society with chivalrous generosity by Bishop Selwyn, when that society laid claim to prior occupation. The bishop knew that there was more than enough unoccupied ground further north. The same spirit of Christian courtesy made Bishop Selwyn (the younger) give up the Island of Mai, in the New Hebrides, to the Presbyterians about 1880, though we had occupied it for some years. The bishop followed in his father's steps, and wished to avoid all disputes. The Presbyterians had occupied Ambrym, which is to the north of Mai, and it was amicably arranged that Ambrym should be the northern boundary of the Presbyterian Mission. The Melanesian Mission works on only three islands in the New Hebrides —Aurora, Pentecost, and Leper's Island. From this southern boundary it stretches its arms at present as far as Ysabel, in the Solomons, but soon, please God, Choiseul and Bougainville shall "hear the joyful sound," and be claimed for Christ's kingdom. New Georgia also awaits conquest in the same Sacred Name.

A story is told of the way in which the first Bishop Selwyn came to visit Melanesia. In his letters patent his jurisdiction was stated as extending as far as thirty-four degrees north latitude. This, it is said, was an error for thirty-four degrees south latitude. But the bishop accepted the position and determined to explore, as soon as he could, islands utterly unknown to missionaries, and only visited by sandal-wood traders and others, who bore, too often, the worst of reputations. Deeds done by white men to the blacks in those days are a disgrace to our nation. An immense improvement has now been effected; let us throw a veil over the past, and attempt rather to make what reparation we can in the name of Him who made of one blood all nations, and commanded us to preach His Gospel to all without distinction.

In 1847 the bishop made his first attempts northward—six years after his arrival in New Zealand. Soon afterwards, after a cruise in dangerous and unchartered waters in a little yacht of twenty-seven tons, *The Undine*, he brought back his first Melanesian scholars, arriving with them in the middle of the night at his little house at

Auckland. Thus we come into contact with St. John's College, Auckland, a sort of school started by the bishop for every one who needed instruction. Here it was that the first Maori clergy were trained. Lady Martin, in her book on the Maoris, tells us of some of the earliest converts. Stephen, the Maori, was dying. He was asked, "What part have you chosen?" He answered, "Christ have I chosen." "Is your heart dark?" "No, it is all light." "Are you suffering much?" "No, no pain, no sadness. This is my desire, that I may go to God, and that my dwelling in this evil world may cease."

On another occasion Rota, the first Maori deacon, came back to St. John's College, after having been eighteen months in charge of a school. On arriving at the college, he said, "I have come to fill my seed bags again, having sown all I took down with me last year."

To this Christian home and school in one the first Melanesians came about the year 1849.

But it may be asked, why did the bishop bring these people away from their own countries? Why did he not scatter white clergymen in the groups of islands at once, following the plan invariably adopted by most missionary societies? The question is natural, and the answer is of the utmost importance. For the bishop's action gave a tone to the Mission which it has never lost. It holds a unique position among all the missions to the heathen throughout the world.

The bishop discovered that the islands untouched as yet by any missions were numbered by dozens rather than by units. To supply them adequately with English clergy was an impossibility. The climate he also considered to be unfit for Europeans as permanent residences, since the groups with which he was concerned lay nearer the equator than any where work had yet been attempted in the South Seas. Then he rose to the conception which has been the constant ideal of the Mission ever since. The natives themselves must be made to become missionaries to their own people. This idea was to be fostered in every possible manner. The number of the English clergy was to be more select than numerous. "They were to be the white floats to sustain the black net," which was to win the souls in the future in Christ's name. The first step, then, in this method was to obtain boys young enough to be instructed. And it required all the wonderful tact and patience and attractive qualities which the bishop possessed to obtain the consent of parents to carry off one of their children to an unknown land in the company of a white man whom possibly they had only seen for a few minutes once or twice. It is indeed wonderful how the scholars were ever obtained in those early days. God was guiding the Mission, and manifestly helping with His Holy Spirit. Of course it was essential from every point that the boys should leave their homes. Only thus could they be guarded from many evil influences, only thus could their language be learnt. And so to St. John's College came the firstfruits of the Mission. And it is worth recording that the idea of a central school where Melanesians from many islands might live happily together was not obtained from books or from the example of any other Mission. It arose from what seemed a casual visit to the island of Anaiteum, in the New Hebrides. There Bishop Selwyn visited the farm of a sandal-wood trader, a Captain Padden—an excellent man, much respected by the natives, and a kind master to his black labourers. The bishop was so much struck with the order and success of the establishment, that he determined to try the experiment in the name of God and for the enlargement of the kingdom of Christ. Ever afterwards he called Captain Padden his "teacher." I know but little of the details of the early days at St. John's College. Ere many years passed it was felt that a separate establishment must be arranged for the Melanesians, with a clergyman specially attached to this work. It is now that the name of the Rev. John Coleridge Patteson appears. He was one of two men won by Bishop Selwyn in England. The other was Mackenzie, afterwards Bishop of Central Africa. It is remarkable that both men died as martyrs for the cause.

Close to St. John's College there is a quiet bay sheltered from cold winds, called Kohimarama. This was purchased chiefly by the profits arising from the sale of the "Daisy Chain," a gift to the Mission by Miss Yonge, the authoress. Here Patteson installed himself, and no one with his heart in missions will ever visit Kohimarama without emotion. The very name was an omen of success, for it means, "the gathering in of light."

A few hundred yards below the house of Mr. Atkin, an old resident, and the father of the Rev. Joseph Atkin, martyred at Nukapu, a quiet bay with a curving shore lies at the feet of the visitor. Not a hundred yards from the water's edge a few plain wooden buildings are visible, prosaic enough to the uninstructed, but eloquent with memories to the Christian heart. One of these is the dormitory where Patteson wrestled in prayer for his beloved Melanesians, and in company with Palmer and Pritt, and other devoted workers, nursed the islanders through a fearful epidemic of dysentery. Six died, in spite of all possible care. God took them as the firstfruits of Melanesia. There, too, stand the little dwellings of the clergy, and the school-house. In the plain grass plot in front two Norfolk Island pines are flourishing. These were planted on the day of Bishop Patteson's consecration. May they live and expand their branches as apt emblems of the spread of Christ's Church in Melanesia! As I looked upon them on a still and beautiful afternoon, in company with a sympathetic friend, I bethought me of the island home of the Mission whence these trees came, and then of numberless coral fringed shores, which once echoed back the noise of incessant battles, but now have grown familiar with the sounds of Christian hymns, and with the aspect of men, unchanged, indeed, so far as native customs are concerned, but transformed by the Holy Spirit into men of peace. And as we lingered, and looked back again and again upon Kohimarama, the seed plot of the harvest already being reaped, my comrade spoke with deep emotion of Patteson, and of his saintly character. "He was a lovely man!" he exclaimed. "He was like the Apostle John." No mission has ever been blessed with two men more remarkable than Selwyn and Patteson, and Selwyn soon was to follow. Perhaps their very dissimilarity of character drew them together. Whole-hearted in their devotion to their Master, and gifted far above the mass of men, they can never be forgotten in the annals of Melanesia. They in time were to be succeeded by Selwyn, the younger, whose praise is in the churches.

Delightful stories are told by Lady Martin of the first arrivals from the islands. When the Melanesians saw two Australian blacks, they looked at them in doubt, and shook their heads, saying, "No good—too black." When the first Melanesian girls arrived at Kohimarama, they knew only two English words—"Ready about." It was not hard to detect the fact that they had been at sea. Soon they picked up a few more words, and were of course glad to make use of them. One day they came into the sitting-room before the lamp was lighted in the evening, and they said, "What, all in the dark, hurrah!"

A neighbour lived close by with a comfortable house, but he was unmarried. One day the girls came back from his house, saying, "Man, money, house, no wife!" They could not understand so strange a state of things.

I notice in the reports that during 1857-8 there were thirty-two Melanesians in New Zealand, speaking six languages. One day a boy pricked himself with an arrow, but said nothing to any one. After a week tetanus set in and he died.

Both Selwyn and Patteson saw that the boys required delicate handling. There was in them all the strength of passionate uncontrolled natures. Yet they had delicate constitutions. The problem to solve was whether they were able to receive by education the energy and perseverance of inhabitants of more temperate climes. I believe the conclusion they came to was that though they could be raised a great deal, yet it was impossible to make a black man into a white man. It was a revelation, however, to all how much could be done by prayerful, godly men, wholly devoted to the work. All idea of the New Zealand school as being like an English school must be set aside. There were no long hours of study. Probably two and a half hours was the utmost ever attempted in a day—and this was divided into two parts.

Indeed, there were more important lessons to

be learnt at first than reading and writing. Perhaps the best method to make the problem really interesting is for my readers to suppose that they have had given into their charge a few untutored Melanesians straight from their heathen homes. Knowing only their heathen customs, what plan should be adopted? The wise founders of this Mission saw that the education of their charges lay more directly in their passage from idleness and dirt to cleanliness and diligence and method than by learning to read and write. The point aimed at was the general effect to be obtained affecting their habits and modes of life. It was a new delight to watch how by degrees a sense of something wanting in themselves was created. It was a great step when they first saw that there was something better than idling, and untidiness, and thoughtlessness. Every day the training, both in social and in religious advancement, continued. The great point to bear in mind was never to disassociate the two sides of education. Improvement in diligence and orderliness went hand in hand with knowledge of the Heavenly Father. Thus, when a lad first arrived at Rohimarama, he found a system with which all were content. Some were cooks; some were gardeners; all did something for the common good. Usually all employments were taken in turn by all, so that each lad knew habits which would be useful to him afterwards. Most of all, he discovered that the bishop and the clergy were not his taskmasters but his fellow-workers. No work was asked of a Melanesian that was not willingly done by one of the clergy—and if the bishop did not spend the days in scrubbing or cooking, they had the sense to know that it was because he could do many things they could not attempt, and devoted himself accordingly to these. The spirit of the establishment made the whites and blacks not only fellow-workers, but brothers. They were bound together by ties of affection. The private room of the clergyman was ever open to any Melanesian lad if he wished to be quiet or to say his prayers. But above all they were taught that they were to be the teachers of their people. This was kept continually before them. They were receiving blessings which they, more than any, must take back to their villages. The following is a specimen of Patteson's teaching : "'When God willed to teach Israel, what way did He take?—He sent prophets to them one after the other. And when Saul, the persecutor, was struck blind at Damascus, how did God teach him?—By sending Ananias to him. And when Cornelius wished for teaching, who was sent to him?—Peter. Now, you are here receiving teaching about the Saviour of the world, who, do you suppose, must teach your people in the islands?' Then they looked at each other, and said softly, 'I suppose we must teach them.'" I have dwelt at length upon this point because it is the foundation principle upon which the work of the Mission is built. Only by realizing it fully will those who are interested in this Mission be able to enter into the problems which I wish to state to them regarding the development of the Mission in the future. The creation of native teachers and of native clergy has been the effort from the first—not a matter to be looked forward to some day, but to be the instrument from the very beginning. For this reason the English clergy do not remain in the islands throughout the year ; but as much responsibility as possible is thrown upon the natives, whilst the clergy return to the central school to take part in the instruction of fresh bands of future teachers whom the Mission ship has landed. It is evident that too much care cannot be given to the training of those who are soon to stand by themselves. Possibly a boy on his return from Norfolk Island may be the only Christian in the village until he can influence others. The deepest spirituality, the most steady zeal, combined with affection and wisdom, are needed. And when a boy has advanced sufficiently in his studies, the question then arises whether he has the gift for teaching others. The only method for discovering this is to set him over portions of the central school, and to watch and to direct him. It is not enough to have zeal and earnestness; a teacher must have capacity as well. How happy and peaceful those days at Kohimarama must have been to those scholars can be gathered from the stories told by the clergy of their charges as they took long walks into the country, or went into Auckland. They would sometimes say, "How pleasant this is!" "How quiet it is!" They were contrasting their present life of freedom from dangers with the old homes, where no one dared move from his house without his arms, and even with them he would not trust himself more than a few hundred yards in the bush for fear of some concealed enemy.

CHAPTER II.

NORFOLK ISLAND.

Norfolk Island, August 19th, 1892.*

IT is but six days since we landed on this most lovely island. But it seems as though I had known it for years. Every hour of each day, and of every evening, has been full to overflowing of new interest and most thrilling associations. Perhaps I had better give my readers a general account of each day's work in order. We landed on Saturday, August 13th, at 11 a.m., at the Cascades, after a passage from Auckland of five days. The only real discomfort upon our journey was the feeling that the ladies on board, who were coming back to the Mission, were suffering a good deal. There is, of course, no stewardess on the ship; nor upon a Mission vessel can you expect aught but the simplest food; and I felt thankful when their troubles were over and we reached the land. The beach was covered with the remains of whales, nor was it necessary to use the eyes to note the fact. The nose told us all that was

* This letter is inserted just as it was written to friends.

needful. Most hearty were the greetings, both from the members of the Mission and from the Norfolk Islanders. The Revs. J. Palmer and A. Brittain, and Mr. Forrest were there, and many ladies. Soon we were driving up through scenery more grateful to the eye than it is easy to express, after our five days at sea. The greenest of green grass stretched away on each side up the slopes of hills; and pines were dotted about in clumps, making the scene very like that of a well-kept English park. But there were shrubs at our side which told of warmer latitudes—bananas, wild tobacco, arum lilies, were in abundance. And in time we came to groves of lemons, covered with fruit, and tree ferns forming avenues right and left. Lemons ripen here all through the year, and are at the disposal of everybody. Guavas were not in season, but the trees formed part of the landscape, and with the handsome "white oaks" completed a glorious scene. It was a lovely day; there was blue sky overhead, and a balmy air, warm and invigorating, was just making itself felt. After three miles of such scenery we approached the Mission buildings, driving down the long pine avenue planted in convict days. Soon we were looking with eager eyes upon what we had heard so much of before—the houses of the clergy, the chapel, the barns, and workshops, dining-hall, etc., and everywhere the Melanesians were watching the bishop and taking note of his peculiarities, height, nose, etc. They seemed interested in many things. The chapel has three most striking features. Its painted glass is quite first rate—at the east end four windows in the apse, the four evangelists, executed by Burne Jones and Morris. At the west end a rose window, and underneath it Philip baptizing the eunuch. The floor is all marble

Interior of St. Barnabas', Norfolk Island.

throughout, and is a glorious piece of work, especially the richer part of it near the altar. The font is of Devonshire marble, and most striking in its warm, rich colours, beautifully blended. The reredos is of Mosaic, and quite lights up the church. That evening I attended the usual evening prayers in Mota, having first received the new member of the Mission—the Rev. W. Browning—by saying a few words to him from the altar steps, and then Mr. Palmer adapted the Ember collects, speaking in Mota. No one has ever failed to be thrilled by the first experience of service in St. Barnabas' Chapel. Behind me, playing the organ with vigour and much feeling, was John Pantutun, a Melanesian. All down the chapel, which is arranged as a college chapel, were some hundred and seventy Melanesians, reverent in demeanour, and singing and repeating responses as one body. English chants and tunes are used. A long solemn pause comes after prayers are finished, while every head is bowed in silent prayer. Then, as noiselessly as they come in, they file out—the girls first, then the Mission party, then the boys. If you are not paying attention you find the church full which you saw empty just before, and it empties just as silently. The bare feet on the marble floor make no sound whatever. Every morning at 7 a.m., and every evening at 7 p.m., the whole family—for it is just a family—meets for worship—Matins and Evensong. Most helpful it is, and it seems to impart that sober, devotional, soothing tone to the day which Churchmen love more and more, when it can be had. Meals are taken in the hall. The centre table is for the Mission party, including any Melanesian deacon or priest. The boys and girls sit at smaller tables all down each side. It may be as well to say here, once for all, that the terms boy and girl stand for Melanesians of any age. One of them here now is grey haired, and was with Patteson when he was killed. Many of the girls are married, and are mothers. The married couples live in little cottages composed of two rooms each. Each couple has one room only. All meals are taken in common in hall. The cooking is very well managed. At present the boys are divided into nine sets, and they take a week each in turn. There are some dozen boys in each gang. These sets sit together at separate tables, and preserve their unity for other purposes —as, for instance, at drill—as sections of a company. They are little cooking brotherhoods in reality, and their sets are made up by mutual agreement. Every day at the common meal one of the tables is seen to be empty, because the cooks who sit there are at work for the week. When we enter at 7.30 a.m., 1 p.m., and 6 p.m. for meals, we see the food for the Melanesians all ready in their plates, and the table is laid for us all. The Melanesians have great plates of rice with a pile of brown sugar in the middle, or else porridge; or at dinner, yams or sweet potatoes, or occasionally meat. As they have but one course, it is an excellent plan, adopted by the Mission staff only, to have their meat in hall. Then they adjourn to one or other of the houses, three times a week, for a pudding, or cake, or tea—all simple and homely. The cooks have to get up sometimes as early as 4 a.m. to get their work done. But this is of no consequence to Melanesians. They sleep on mats, which in the daytime are rolled up and put on a shelf. Each set of cooks cuts its own firewood, and has it ready before its cooking week comes. At present it is once in every nine weeks. After breakfast there is school for an hour and a half, and then the boys are told off to their different kinds of farm work and cleaning up. After dinner there is school till three, when play begins till six; and after evening chapel, at 7 p.m., there is an hour more school. It will be seen that not much intellectual strain is put upon the boys. They learn to read and write and sum. And they learn how to keep houses clean, and how to farm, and milk, and feed cattle, etc. In fact they are taught to fill the place which a man reclaimed from heathenism and savagery ought to lead within the tropics. No one expects the vigour amongst them seen in white races in temperate regions. It would be absurd to expect it. The best and steadiest scholars become teachers with small salaries—about five pounds a year—and some are finally ordained. Everything is done to make them depend upon themselves, and not upon the white man. But the staff here, of course, supervise and help in everything. One is head cook; another farms, and looks after the roads.

The roads near the Mission are kept in order by the Mission, and they are a credit to our community. The girls live in their rooms, attached to the houses of the married clergy. Where I am staying—at Mr. and Mrs. Palmer's—there are, I think, eleven. They are like members of the family, and help in all household matters. And, of course, they are taught sewing. I believe they are all betrothed, and in some cases their future husbands are here too. But etiquette is very strict, and they seldom meet. Probably it is difficult to break down these customs here, even to a reasonable extent, because the parents might object. These girls very often slip past my window, which opens on to a verandah. They never seem to quarrel. Indeed, the whole community is a pattern in this respect. The boys sit in the rooms of the unmarried clergy and can go into their bed-rooms at any time to be quiet. And, of course, the chapel doors stand open day and night. If a boy is ill you will find him generally stretched on the floor in one of the sitting-rooms. As I am discoursing upon such details of ordinary life, perhaps this will be the best place to insert an account of a cricket match. On Tuesday, August 16, we had a cricket match, for be it known to all that it is always holidays while the *Southern Cross* is here. Holidays begin at the moment when the first lucky boy espies the ship, and cries, "Sail oh!" The cry is echoed most musically from farm to farm, and hill to hill, and soon the whole island knows that tidings from the great world outside can once more be expected. Happy island! Here, Ireland is hardly known by name. The wars and rumours of strife in Parliament, or battle field, are of little consequence here. The boy who first sees the ship gets a shilling, and the community storms down to the shore, watching first to see on which side of the island the ship can anchor. But to return to the cricket match. The sides were to be those who were going back this voyage *versus* those who were staying here. My side had first innings, and I went in first, not expecting to see much science among the bowlers. I was, however, speedily undeceived. The first ball, pitched well, broke from leg, and nearly took my off stump. The next was equally well pitched, and hit my thumb; the next took the middle finger. There was no doubt about it that the Melanesians could bowl really well, and at a great pace. I was soon caught in the outfield, and went away to bowl to my own side, and to practise catching in a corner of the ground, very much impressed with the

Cricketers at St. Barnabas', Norfolk Island.

capacity of my boys. They are not, as a rule, good bats, because they have had no training, and only a few catch well yet. But one or two showed capital form with the ball. One in particular—Samuel Sagler—timed some shooters in a style which was worthy of any eleven, and hit out at pitched up balls like a man. John Pantutun also, the organist, is a really good cricketer. I feel sure that they and one or two others, could be trained up to good English county eleven standard. It was the first time that I had seen barefooted cricketers. One envied them their hold of the ground, and also I envied them the hardness of their shins. They did not seem to feel blows I should have strongly objected to, for the bowling was above medium pace. We all picnicked together on the grass, and then photographs were taken.

Let me now describe my first Sunday—a day never to be forgotten—filled to the full with deepest interest. In the morning, after Matins in Mota, there was a celebration of Holy Communion in English, and I celebrated. How full the church seemed of sacred memories—of the work of the Selwyns, Patteson, and of many, past and present, whose names are written in the book of life! After dinner I drove to the old township—the centre of the old convict settlement. We passed all along the pine avenue, which is on a kind of plateau, and a mile broad; then, turning to the left, down a valley green with grass, we followed a road quite steep in places, till we came to the sea, passing the old watermill, which has unfortunately been permitted to tumble all to pieces. At length the prison buildings came into view. Of course, there is a general likeness between them and those at Port Arthur—the same massive walls and look of strength. But the resemblance is only general.

The ground is more open here, and the buildings form a larger group. The commissariat store house, the barracks and officers' quarters are really fine buildings, and the governor's house overlooks the prison buildings, which are now in complete ruin, though the outer walls are standing. In the old commissariat store we held our confirmation. The long room was packed with Norfolk Islanders, and I must have been dull indeed not to have felt strongly the interest of the scene, and not to have recalled a strange history as I read out the names of Nobbs and Quintal, and Christian and Buffet and Young. Thirty-seven were confirmed. Before I began my address I could not help referring to the connection which subsisted in old days between Tasmania and Norfolk Island, and that my own feelings were deeply stirred now that for the first time since the Norfolkers had arrived a Bishop of Tasmania stood among them. The welcome and the kindness which I have received from this community has been unbounded. The same evening (Sunday evening) I confirmed fifteen Melanesians in their own church. I have not been so anxious for years about any service as I was on this occasion. I had to preach through an interpreter, and those who have not tried it hardly know how difficult it is. The interpreter also needs our sympathy! Mr. Palmer gallantly stood by me and supported me. But the most agitating part was still to come. I had to read the service in Mota. Even if I had learnt the language it would have been anxious work to speak before the Mission staff and all the boys and girls. But, considering I had not learnt the language, and that I wished to acquit myself well, it was for me a memorable occasion. On Tuesday morning, at 8 a.m., the church was again filled to overflowing, on the occasion of the ordination of William Moreton Vaget as a deacon. As the morning dawned we saw that it would be another lovely day, and soon parties on horseback were arriving from various parts, specially invited to take part in the service. Mr. Palmer preached the sermon, and found it all he could do to tell us in simple language, first in English, then in Mota, of his early days in Merelava, where William Vaget was brought up, and of his joy at seeing him stand there to become an ordained clergyman to his own people. Vaget has earned a good report as a thoroughly consistent and faithful Christian, and goes back with us to build up the Church in his own island. The offertory was given to him for his church. A sum of nearly five pounds was collected, and he is going to spend it in lamps for the church. He answered the questions firmly, and then I laid my hands upon him. He read the Gospel and helped in the administration of Holy Communion. My second service in Mota did not agitate me so much, and yet it was a great strain. The whole congregation breakfasted together afterwards, and on this day it was that we had our cricket match, William playing on my side. That evening William read the evening prayer in church, another boy reading the lessons. How can I make my readers realize the happy home life here among the Mission staff—the many talks, the unity of purpose which makes all hearts one, the sense of reality of all one sees of simple Christian life, the thought that the scholars here are the raw material by which the multitude of the isles shall know Christ and become his disciples? This, and much more. The precincts of the buildings are so like a piece of beautiful England—shady trees, green grass, the church bell, the church clock, the sound of organ and many voices, make one think of a place much to be desired for one's soul's good. Yet this is but the centre of work for hundreds of islands. Here the clergy come to rest and still to work—worn, and often sick, after months of loneliness. Here, also, the wives wait for months without tidings from their husbands, drawn all the more closely together by their common anxieties, drawn closer to God, too, by the need for His all-loving care. They all did me the honour to ask me to address them specially in the church one evening; but how gladly would I have sat and learnt from them! On another evening they collected all the heads of families in the island to give me a welcome. And then I was asked to speak at a great meeting on the old township, and gladly did so, telling them of Tasmania. Last, not least, I inspected the schools and examined all the children, and then passed on to visit the aged Mrs. Nobbs, who still lives, much respected by all.

The *Southern Cross* starts in an hour, and I cannot leave this place without recording my thankfulness to God for having brought me here to help, in however little a degree, a work so blessed by God. I feel that if only our people knew what I now know, their hearts would open to help these workers in a degree which at present they have not realized. With all my heart I hope to try and make others form some conception of one of the very noblest missions of the Church of England. Not even does New Zealand realize this work, though the Bishop of Melanesia is in the New Zealand province. I believe I shall have to tell my readers when I see them again that the money yearly given must increase by thousands if the area of the work is to be adequately covered.

May God prosper the *Southern Cross* on her voyage, and bring back the workers to their homes here again in peace. Above all, may God put it into the hearts of those who are to choose the new bishop to send the man best fitted to undertake one of the most inspiring posts in the world. Norfolk Island is, externally, a little paradise. But to me there is a greater and more perfect loveliness enshrined in the work and aims and quiet Christian life of the friends among whom I have been living.

Thus had I written on the eve of my departure. It is with heartfelt sorrow that I had to record the death, a month or two after we sailed, of Mrs. Palmer, my kind hostess and friend. No one who knew her could fail to reverence her bright and noble nature. She was a blessing to her husband, to her children, and to the community; a peacemaker, an inspirer of others to continue in well-doing. It was she who, at the last moment, implored her husband to accompany me. It was her hand that I shook last on embarking as she wished us God speed. Her husband returned full of happy anticipations as Norfolk Island rose upon the horizon; but only to find that his wife had been in her grave many weeks. It was a sad home-coming.

CHAPTER III.

THE NORFOLK ISLANDERS—THEIR CUSTOMS AND LANGUAGE.

CHAPTER may profitably be devoted to that interesting community to whom Norfolk Island belongs—the ex-Pitcairn Islanders. They have their own laws and customs, and from them the Melanesian mission bought its farm.

They came to Norfolk Island in 1856, headed by their clergyman, the Rev. Mr. Nobbs; and they are, as is well known, the offspring of the mutineers of the *Bounty* and of Tahitian women.

Those who know anything of half-caste races can easily draw up a fairly correct list of virtues and vices inherent in a race of such mixed blood as this, and it is not incumbent upon me to attempt the task here. It is sufficient to say that it would be difficult to find anywhere a more pleasant, laughter-loving, hospitable people than the Norfolk Islanders of this day. There can be no doubt, however, and I think the thoughtful among them realize it, that the effect of constant intermarriage within so small a community has had a serious effect already in deterioration of the race, physically and mentally. It is a matter which calls for immediate attention in a sympathetic and liberal minded spirit. The community is ruled by a governor, that governor being also Governor of New South Wales, and it is the smallest crown colony in the world. There is reason to suppose that ere long the New South Wales Government will station there a governor chosen from outside. The governor has a seal, appoints judges, and can sell or allocate waste lands. The laws are framed as far as possible on the model of those which were in force in Pitcairn Island. The actual government is in the hands of a chief magistrate and two councillors, elected annually. The chief magistrate must be a landed proprietor and over twenty-eight years of age. The councillors must be at least twenty-five. The annual election is on the 25th of December. The chaplain presides, and the proceedings open with prayer. All can vote who have resided six months on the island, are twenty years of age, and can read and write. The chaplain has a casting vote, but he cannot be either magistrate or councillor. The officers can summon to their aid, in case of necessity, any one in the island, on penalty of a fine for non-attendance. The chief magistrate is expressly ordered to attempt to settle all quarrels out of court. If this is impossible he may fine up to fifty shillings without appeal. The highest fine he can inflict is ten pounds. If the parties are unwilling to abide by his decision, a jury of seven is empanelled, and their decision is final. Offences of a more serious nature are sent for trial to Sydney. It is interesting to note that the jury is entitled to payment, and that one hour is computed at one-eighth of a day's work. As a rule fines are worked out in labour on the roads or elsewhere. A list of all males over twenty-five is kept, and these are called elders. When a jury is needed the names are put into a bag, and the first seven drawn out compose the jury for the occasion. The rules regarding education are strict. The children must attend school from the age of six to fourteen. If any child is absent for more than two days on account of sickness the chaplain must certify the fact. The fine for non-attendance at school is sixpence per day. Each child pays a school fee of ten shillings per annum. This and the fines for non-attendance go to the schoolmaster. (From which it would appear that, if only the master could induce all his charges to absent themselves, his post would be a distinctly lucrative one.) The school is under the care of the chaplain. No intoxicating liquors are permitted, not even (there is a touch of irony in this) to the chaplain. The rule in its breadth is, I believe, rigidly enforced. There is a fine for using profane language, ranging from five to forty shillings. No furious riding or driving is permitted on the roads. No person may sell land to any one who has not obtained the consent of the governor previously.

The population now consists of about six hundred and fifty on Norfolk Island, and there are a hundred and twenty-five more who are still at Pitcairn Island, they or their parents having returned of their own accord to their old home. At the present time there are some twenty (not more) who may be called pure half-castes. Of this number is, of course, the aged Mrs. Nobbs, who still lives, the wife of the well-known clergyman. A few remarks on the language of the Norfolk Islanders will create interest, and I am anxious to record the derivations of some extraordinary words which are now well known, but which the next generation will use without any idea how they were coined.

First, there are in common use some definitely Tahitian words which present no difficulty, but sound strangely. "Wa-a-wa-ha" is one of these, meaning disgusting. The derivation of "sullun" and "utlun" is more obscure, meaning "the people" and "all the people;" though in Melanesia I have met the word "sul," the people. You do not in this favoured isle say "very odd" but "sem-is-ways." If a person is saying farewell you would not say "I am very sorry," but "I mussa buss for sorrow for you." A crying person is a "myosullun," and if something were dropping to pieces you would say it was "wa-oo-loo."

But the words which I specially wish to fix as curiosities are of another sort. There is one serious danger in paying a visit to these people, especially if there is anything peculiar in your habits or appearance. It is more than likely that your surname may be permanently incorporated into the language as an adjective denoting that peculiarity. This is at least alarming. The course alluded to has been adopted sufficiently often to warrant incurring a serious risk in the case of any future visitor. For instance, it is now a common phrase among this community to say, "I shall big Jack," meaning "I shall cry." This phrase is derived from an actual person, Mr. John Evans, who is a stout man and addicted to tears. His softness of disposition has added a word to the language. Another phrase is a "Corey sullun," meaning "a busybody." A Mr. Corey, a visitor here, was reputed to be a busybody, and he has in consequence enriched this curious language with a new adjective. Still more strange is it when such epithets are added to the names of four-footed animals. "That is a Breman cow," you may hear a man say. Now, poor Mr. Breman was also a casual visitor, and was remarkably thin. The fact that he was a stranger called attention to his personal appearance, and "Breman" now stands for "thin," and probably will continue to do so for ever, or till some thinner person attracts their notice. From the action of the same law, "a Snell sullun" is a niggardly man. I have said enough to call attention to a most curious evolution of language arising from the extreme rarity of communication between the outer world and their harbourless island. A new face excites general astonishment, and close observation leads to the enrichment of the language at the expense of the individual.

The children are particularly good-looking and very shy. On one occasion, as I was walking down the pine avenue, I saw several children hiding behind a tree, and keeping the trunk of it between myself and them, and as soon as I had passed they fled like deer in the opposite direction. In speaking, all these people have a peculiar drawling intonation, not at all unpleasant, however, in the mouths of persons with such soft and musical voices. A friend tells me that one night he was returning home in the dark, and overheard the following conversation between two parties of Norfolkers. A shout from the first party, "Who's you!" Answer, "I's me!" Even little facts like these help to bring before our readers this interesting community.

The great need for them is a magistrate from outside. At present, as they are all related, the magistrate is uncle or cousin to every soul amongst them, and it must be hard indeed for the embodiment of the law to resist the pleadings of his relations. It is a pleasant thing to know that the late Sir Robert Duff took the warmest interest in this community. Had he lived he would have made a determined effort to improve their condition.

CHAPTER IV.

LIFE ON BOARD THE "SOUTHERN CROSS."

A WITTY person in the early days of the Melanesian Mission made the remark that Bishop Selwyn was a man "fond of yachting."

The idea thus expressed is so ludicrous when applied to life on the Mission ship that it cannot but provoke a smile. But if it seems absurd to myself, cognizant only with the details of the latest, and by far the most comfortable, of the ships that have been in use, what must have been the truth in the early days? Verily a man must have possessed a head and a stomach of some stout metallic substance to have braved the experiences of the *Undine* in Bishop Selwyn's early days. She was, I believe a little vessel of about twenty-three tons. In this craft he cruised in unknown waters, chartless, and full of dangers. The shores everywhere contained people who had either never seen a white man, or only knew him as represented by the type of the too often brutal and merciless trader of old. To those who know what the heat of these regions is, and how welcome

Captain Bongard of the "Southern Cross."

is a little space to permit of pure air, it will be a wonderful thing to remember that the bishop sailed his own vessel, and came home with dozens of Melanesians packed into his little cabins. The *Undine* was succeeded by several vessels, until in 1891 the new *Southern Cross* was built in England, costing ten thousand pounds, and arranged specially for the work which she has to do. She is about three hundred tons register, with an auxiliary engine which propels her at about six knots. She has also three masts, the foremast being rigged with square yards. The accommodation for the clergy is on deck; there is a saloon with a table about twelve feet long; along each side are three bunks; and just aft of the saloon are two little cabins. It will be seen, therefore, that eight people can be accommodated with berths. A mattress is provided in each of these, but nothing else. Each clergyman brings his own pillow and rug, and takes them with him when he lands, and of course he makes his own bed tidy every morning. We used to be highly amused with one of our number who had a good many possessions. He seemed to lie down first at night, and then he fitted round him in the remaining available space, baskets, billys, bags, etc. Naturally we used to admire his ingenuity, though we were unable to imitate it. As regards meals, a cup of coffee is served at six, breakfast at eight, lunch at twelve, and dinner at five. These meals were of the simplest. There was plenty of food in the shape of soup, tinned meat, rice, and yams, and tea and coffee to drink. Sometimes we had fowls—ancient bipeds many of them were, who, without doubt, had tramped countless miles through this weary world; they were bought for a stick of tobacco, a price that is something less than a halfpenny. Were they really cheap? I am not quite sure that they were, except for soup. But who can tell the joy that was experienced by the community when some one furtively produced a bottle of lemon syrup! A present most likely from some of the ladies at Norfolk Island. Warm were the offers of friendship made to the lucky possessor. There were also days, of course, when ship's plum-pudding — immense, globular, and spotted with raisins—made its triumphant entrance, and there were two sauces always at hand—hunger, and the laughter ready to greet jokes, which were ceaseless. But it would be invidious were I to indicate the special jesters. At ten o'clock every morning daily prayers in Mota are said, usually in the large "schoolroom," as it is termed—that is, the space below the deck where the Melanesians ate and slept. There were three of these rooms—two for the boys forward, one for the girls aft—with separate staircases. Of course, all the clergy attend prayers, and the Canticles and Glorias are sung, as well as a hymn. At 7 p.m. English prayers are said in the saloon, attended by the crew who are not on watch, and by the clergy. Directly afterwards there followed Evensong for the Melanesians. On Sundays a morning service for Europeans at ten o'clock was added. And whenever it was practicable there was a celebration of Holy Communion on Sundays at seven a.m. in the saloon. But naturally, if we were at anchor, all services were ashore, except for the crew.

Let us imagine that we are approaching some island. It is arranged that one of the clergy shall take the boat in. The steer oar is always taken by one of the clergy. The boat's crew of Melanesians is ordered out, usually the same boys, and then the boat is lowered and rows away, whilst the captain hangs off and on, waiting till the work is done. "The skipper," as he is familiarly termed, is a man of divine temper, otherwise this process of waiting and watching, often for hours after the time fixed, would have driven him distracted. Coral reefs appear on every hand, and constant care has to be exercised. It is very hard to fix a definite time for the return. Perhaps a boy has to be fetched; but first he has to say farewell to a whole village, or else he is at his garden a couple of miles off, and has to be sent for, or there would be a dozen other reasons for delay. It is to be noted also that the crews of boats going ashore are always Melanesians. On no single occasion did the white sailors go ashore during her trip. And the reason is obvious. First, they are wanted on board; secondly, they might do something or say something which might end in a serious quarrel. Upon the return of the boat there is a rush to the ropes, and twenty Melanesians soon bring her up to the davits. The actual landing often possesses interest. Sometimes it is a question of wading over fifty yards of sharp coral while the boat is held by men in a deep channel in the reef, as at Ureparapara. Sometimes it is necessary to wait for a big wave, and row right over the steep edge of a reef, and come fairly down on the flat portion, whilst the natives are there to pull the boat further up, and we all jump out—as, for example, at Te Motu, in Santa Cruz. More often there is a shallow shore. But woe betide those who have cuts or bruises on their legs—and it is hard to prevent them coming—for this constant wading in salt water pickles the wounds, and prevents them from closing.

But there is one department of work on board the vessel which is most trying, and of which I had heard nothing till I saw it with my own eyes.

It must be understood that the native teachers in the islands have to be paid their salaries once a year. Usually, for example, the Solomons are taken during one voyage and the Banks in the next. Let me describe, then, what this process means. Months before the time of delivery the teachers have notified their wants, and the goods have been bought in Auckland and stored on the vessel. There the clergy work in the hold—hot with tropical sun and close contact with Melanesian bodies. At one of our stages I remember that we had to pay thirty-five teachers, a simple business if it meant a sum of money; but it becomes a serious business when it means payment in a multifarious collection of household necessities. The list of possible wants was portentously long. It included, I remember, shirts, axes, biscuits, soap, candles, tobacco, matches, calico, trousers, tinned meat, tea, pipes, saucepans, kettles, *et hoc genus omne*. (I always watched the bars of yellow soap going into the boat with the secret hope that one might go overboard and be swallowed by a shark as a soothing pill.) How often I have felt genuine sympathy for the clergy, as on a hot and sweltering day they have emerged from the hold, having in the last few hours acted the part of a grocer, ironmonger, draper, and tobacconist. Two articles are notably absent from the list. I believe the clergy would go into fits if they were asked for either boots or stockings. It is supposed that these do not exist anywhere in these latitudes. How often I have seen (also with sympathy) these same clergy throw themselves down in the saloon to get a quarter of an hour's nap after the process above mentioned. This is the yachting of which the clergy of the Melanesian Mission are so passionately fond. There were times, of course, when the day's work was done, and the sun had gone to rest, and the ship was at anchor in some quiet bay; then a sense of peace stole over our minds, and converse could be free, and range over many subjects. At such times it was permissible even to sit on deck in those suits, light and not elegant, which men find useful as "garments of the night" in the tropics. I recall those happy evenings with genuine pleasure, spent in congenial society, and the discussion of many subjects, both grave and gay.

At certain places the Melanesians who are on board all go ashore, notably at the waterfall on Aurora. The women and girls then usually have a great washing-day and all bathe in the numerous streams that branch out in various places. On board it is hardly possible to do anything in the way of instruction. The interruptions are so frequent and the space so limited that it has been found impracticable, even if there were leisure. The extraordinary good temper of these people is a remarkable fact. Collected from all sorts of islands, compelled to live in a small space, and to eat under difficulties sometimes, I believe there is no case on record of a quarrel amongst them. They are fearless climbers, and will go anywhere on the rigging. Sometimes a party is seen seated on the bowsprit, and a few more on the dolphin striker. Occasionally one or two are stretched asleep on the rail, looking as if they must tumble into the sea. There are instances, indeed, where this has occurred, but without loss of life. The Melanesians have their own cooking galleys, and appoint some of their number as cooks. Yams are plentifully supplied, and rice, and at times other delicacies. The boys come on board decorated with all sorts of earrings and nose rings, but by degrees these disappear. Before they reach

Norfolk Island they have to put on shirts and trousers, and appropriate garments of English pattern are served out to the girls. I believe the scene in the boys' schoolroom is mirth-compelling when the clergy are seen distinguishing the front from the back of a garment, and explaining the use of buttons.

Every Melanesian is, of course, a perfect swimmer. Indeed, they say that the women are even better than the men. It used to be a recognized custom in old days for discontented wives in Mota to swim across to Vanua Lava, a distance of seven miles.

When the ship anchors the Melanesians are quickly over the side, jumping from the bulwarks on the rigging, with a glorious disregard of marine monsters. How we used to envy the manner in which they dried themselves! They simply became dry, their clothes being of the scantiest. The clergy, having a dread of sharks, do not often bathe in the sea. But in the tropical showers that descend so suddenly at intervals, one who ventured to brave the elements on the deck of the Mission vessel might easily meet a reverend gentleman, nay, even a right reverend gentleman, clad in bathing costume walking about in the rain in order to get the much-valued fresh-water bath. I have kept to the lighter details, but of course there is much time for study in the ship on the days when no land is in sight, and such opportunities are utilized to the full. Life in the Mission has many trials, but the ship restores tone to the clergy by bringing congenial spirits together, and by breaking through the monotony of work on shore.

In 1895, during the last voyage, the clergy had a unique experience, which might easily have had fatal results for the ship. Suddenly and without any clear reason, the whole ship's crew, including the captain and mate, were struck down with island fever of a very pronounced type. Fortunately the engineer escaped. The crew resigned themselves to die, their weakness was so great; the captain could just drag himself on deck to take bearings. For weeks the ship was in the hands of the clergy. The Rev. T. C. Cullwick cooked for the entire party; Mr. Comins was specially in charge of the wheel, and the Melanesians were not very numerous. The ship was at length anchored off Norfolk Island, and a crew of Norfolk Islanders took her to Auckland. The young bishop was on board, and was the life and soul of the party.

Now that my readers have gained some idea of the Mission ship, I propose to embark on the story of the long cruise which the writer of these lines entered upon with such deep interest. Some nine hundred miles of water, however, intervene between Norfolk Island and the Northern Hebrides. It will not, therefore, be out of place to insert here a statement of the principles of the Mission in their island work.

In the early days it was the invariable custom for the bishop to land first upon an unknown island, and, as a rule, unaccompanied. Usually the boat was stopped some few yards from the shore, and the chief pastor took a header into the sea and swam ashore, carrying with him a few presents in order to make friends with his flock. Above all, he was anxious to note the names of a few of the people, and to catch a few words of the language. Such discoveries were invaluable upon the occasion of a second visit; and obviously little more than a simple interchange of civilities could be effected at first. In this manner seventy-eight islands were visited in 1857.

I have asked myself what a stranger would expect to see if he were to land now at one of our stations in Melanesia. Those who have never read the records of our mission would certainly expect to be met by a white clergyman, and to be conducted to a well-built house, with broad verandah, and a nicely kept garden, and all the signs of an Arcadian existence—possibly he would expect to see a white lady smiling a welcome, with children at her knee. Nothing of the kind would meet his eye. Only one white lady has ever attempted the tour in the Mission ship, namely, Mrs. Selwyn. Her appearance excited the greatest wonder, and the inquisitiveness of the natives must have been embarrassing. But perhaps the greatest excitement of all was caused by the appearance of a white boy of eight years. Mr. Palmer took one of his children with him on one occasion. The Melanesians could not make enough of this new and delightful specimen of humanity. A visitor to these islands would very likely meet no white clergyman, because there are so few of them, and they are constantly moving about in their whale boats. The ten islands of the Banks Group and the forty-five schools are superintended by one white man. He carries all his worldly possessions, including his tinned meat and tea and biscuit, in his whale boat. In some groups the clergyman's boat, with its native crew, stretches away forty miles in the open sea to gain the next island. A moonlight night is chosen, if possible, because it is cool, and though it seems pleasant to rush along before a steady sea breeze in this manner, it is by no means so delightful to be compelled to beat back against such a persistent wind in an open boat, and one that must be light enough to be easily pulled up upon a reef.

It will be obvious also that the large and comfortable house is also a myth. The clergy have no definite home in these islands. Each centre has a light bamboo erection, resembling a native house, which is kept for the clergyman. The sides are very open, in order to admit as much air as possible. There is a partition in the middle, which enables us to call one part the parlour, and the other the bedroom. There is a raised bamboo platform in one spot; this is the bed, and indicates the bedroom. There is nothing in the other partition; this tells you it is the parlour.

When the clergyman arrives, his people carry up his goods, and he camps out in his bamboo house, arranges his pots and pans, and cooks his food with the assistance of his boys, and also of a collection of all sorts and conditions of people. I used to note that these helpers were naturally wonderfully good assistants when the fragments of the feasts were to be disposed of. Indeed, no Boaz was ever so prodigal in leaving sufficient for the gleaners as the clergy are in thinking of their retainers. It is, of course, a sort of family compact. A crew of boys will accompany the clergyman for a month in his tour; he will feed them; and at the end of the cruise they receive a little tobacco and some calico, and are content. On no other system could men of such limited incomes afford to live at all. The native food is for the most part supplied gratis by the people of the village.

Often as I looked round these simple little bamboo houses, I realized what a lonely feeling might come over a man when he was laid low with a touch of fever—no white faces, no comforts, no soft bed, no one who understood cooking; nothing but his own brave heart and his trust in the Saviour, Whose work he was doing so gallantly to sustain him in the hour of sickness or despondency. And yet it is hardly fair to say no more than this. There would generally be faithful Melanesians whose hearts have been won to Christ, and who love their clergy and would do anything for them.

What our visitor would first see would be a strip of coral strand, overhung with trees of densest green foliage, interspersed with cocoanut palms and bananas, and a few natives standing about in island costume. Possibly a man clad in shirt and trousers would appear soon, and prove to be the native teacher, who would invite him to his house. A hundred yards of track would bring him to a cluster of native houses, with the school or church recognizable by its cross. And here he would obtain a visible proof of what I now proceed to relate—the principle of the Mission in their endeavour to avoid Anglicizing the natives or bringing so much authority to bear upon them as to crush their sense of responsibility.

For instance, what are the relations between one of the clergy and a native chief? Does he destroy his power, or effect the prestige of the head man of the village? There could not be a more important principle to settle; fortunately Bishop Patteson laid down the lines of action in so truly liberal and wise a manner that they have never needed alteration.

There are some misconceptions on the part of a native which are hard to dissipate. For instance, he will persist in believing that a white man can cure every ailment and disease. Of course, experience soon decides this point, and proves the white man right in his assertions. At the same time the clergy do work marvels where they have time to superintend a sick case, for they have on their side that implicit trust in the doctor on the part of the patient which is so well recognized a cause of success.

Again, converts are apt to wish to transfer their allegiance from their chief to their clergyman, but the attempt is stoutly resisted. At the same time it is right to point out clearly that some laws are God's laws, not man's; and if a chief asks a Christian to break one of God's laws he must be resisted; in no other way can a standard of purity, for instance, be sustained.

Sometimes it is a terrible temptation to a clergyman to dictate to his people on many subjects where amendment is most needful, and to force better customs upon them by threats of withdrawal of spiritual privileges if his suggestions are not heeded. It requires great self-restraint to work more slowly, and in the end more surely; for if the teacher attempts to lord it over the people the day will certainly come when he is disliked. The best plan to adopt is to work, in all matters not absolutely essential, through the chief. It is a slower method, but more certain. Who, for instance, is to regulate the price of labour for work done for the white man? May it not be arranged by the clergyman? Ought he not to expect free labour in the building of his house since he has come to do these people good? No; the chief must be urged to make the regulations where there is a chief, and if the native Christians will not give free labour, then they should be cheerfully paid for it. I know that one clergyman, for instance, gives a box of tobacco weighing forty pounds for each of his little houses in his various centres. At the same time, whilst the chief is urged to take his right place, and whilst it is conclusively proved to him that his authority is not to be destroyed upon the advent of "the new teaching," yet, at the same time, he should be advised to consult with those who can give him the best advice.

Where such a line of conduct is not adopted, it is obvious that the chiefs of a neighbouring district would be most unwilling to accept a Christian teacher; indeed, the undermining of a chief's power often leads to the destruction of all authority. People end by obeying no one when they begin by disobeying their chief, and then see that the teacher is not competent to decide many of the questions which in time press for an answer.

There is also another principle which has far-reaching results. Well-meaning Englishmen who have been brought up in a somewhat narrow circle of thought and opinion, are apt to make non-essentials into essentials to the grievous hurt of the great cause. The aim of all missions should be to show that Christ's religion is adapted to the circumstances and customs of all nations and every clime, and no established habits should be interfered with, unless they are directly contrary to the declared will of God. But because this has not been borne in mind, the progress of the Gospel has been very much hindered. The impression has gained ground that natives must change many habits, which, as a matter of fact, are indifferent, neither right nor wrong, or wrong only to excess. Some white teachers in some mission fields, I am told, have a horror of smoking, and make abstinence from this habit virtually a condition of baptism. Others see harm in native dances, or in betel chewing, or in kava drinking. The Melanesian Mission has always taken a clear line in these questions. None of these things are wrong in themselves. Sometimes in the old days native Christians came to Bishop Patteson for an opinion upon such points (one of them referred to dances in secret societies), but he refused to give his opinion. He feared to lay a burden upon them which they were not called upon to bear, through ignorance of the precise facts, and he told them to be guided by their consciences. Our Mission again has no rules as to clothing, except that those who come to school must be decent from the native point of view. As to smoking, I have seen a little girl of eight with a black pipe stuck in her waist band. Betel chewing, and, so far as I know, kava drinking proceed as before. One great cause of rejoicing is that these islanders never seem to have made intoxicants from the palm; and it is needless to say, that we have never attempted to instruct them in these arts.

The first land reached by the *Southern Cross* in its northern journey from Norfolk Island is the group near New Caledonia, called the Loyalty Islands. In Bishop Patteson's days there was a central school established in Lifu, and boys were brought here in place of being transported to Kohimarama. But the Melanesians were not attracted by Lifu. The reason for this suggests that, though Norfolk Island is a very long way from some of our stations, yet it has attractions which are wanting in nearer latitudes.

The boys complained that at Lifu there was "nothing new to see." Who can tell how much the Mission has been aided by the natural instinct of man to see a world of new sights? There was another objection also to this school. "The Lifu people are very kind, but no water, no bread-fruit, no bananas, no fish; very good, go to New Zealand."

Rather than clash with the workers of the London Missionary Society, Bishop Patteson resigned Lifu to this mission. The same is true of another island in the map called Maré. When I landed at Nengone on this island one of the first objects that I noticed was the grave of Mr. Nihill, one of our earliest clergy. The London Missionary Society hold this island now, and the Roman Catholics have a station here as well. We landed solely for the purpose of paying a pension to one of our native clergy, the Rev. M. Wadrokal.

After another long stretch of sea the New Hebrides are reached. Here the Presbyterians are at work. Island after island is passed by the ship until we approach our own stations. One of these southern islands, Mai, was occupied by us up to ten years ago, and it was surrendered at that time to the Presbyterians in order to make our own boundary a perfectly clear one, a little to the north of Mai.

In 1880, the Rev. R. Comins was at Mai. The people were as wild a possible, and there was no small amount of risk in living among them. On one occasion, when the *Southern Cross* was anchored here, the chief was accused of stealing something, and he became very angry. He was then invited on board in order to pacify him; but he was suspicious, and would not consent unless a hostage was left on shore. Comins offered himself, but he confessed that he had an anxious time of it. The men sat round him with their loaded rifles, angry and suspicious, and watching the ship. Had any disturbance been noticed on board he would have been certainly shot. After a while he drew out his sketch book and began drawing. One by one his guards looked over his shoulder, then they began to smile and then to laugh; then they made friends; and when the boat returned all traces of suspicion had vanished. On another occasion when Mr. Comins had been landed and had obtained the help of his people to carry his boxes to the village, the last of these porters found his load a heavy one, and requested Comins to carry his rifle for him. Accordingly the last in the procession was the white man armed with a rifle; and he laughingly said that had he been seen in this position by the correspondent of some newspaper there would have appeared a slashing article setting forth the slave-driving propensities of the Melanesian clergy, who went about armed to the teeth, whilst the natives worked in fear of their lives.

But the most amusing occurrence at Mai has still to be related. One day Mr. Comins was walking along the shore with one of his people. At about a mile off he saw another native, and pointed him out to his companions. "He is one of my enemies," he said.

"Look at him through my glass," replied Comins. The native took up the glass and gazed. Then, in a moment, as he saw the magnified image so much closer than before, he dropped the binocular and grasped his arrows. To his astonishment his enemy had receded once more. Again he looked, more puzzled than ever, and again grasped his weapons. At length a happy thought struck him, "You hold the glasses," he cried eagerly, "and then I can shoot him."

Mr. Comins left Mai with deep regret, for he had learnt the language and had come to know the people.

Three of the Northern Hebrides are in the charge of our Mission—Aurora, Pentecost, and Leper's Island. But I reserve the history of these, and pass on to the group by far the best known of any—the Banks Islands.

CHAPTER V.

THE BANKS GROUP OF ISLANDS.

FORTY-FIVE schools, two thousand two hundred and eighty nine baptized persons; three thousand six hundred and eighty-two attending services; about three thousand heathens. The Rev. George Sarawia is in charge here.

Directly north of the New Hebrides, and at no great distance, a cluster of coral islands appears on the horizon. There are nine of these, excluding some that are very small. Formerly they were inhabited by as savage natives as any in these seas; but the Mission has taken so great a hold here that it is only in Santa Maria and Vanua Lava that any heathens can be said to remain, and these are the two largest islands. Wondrous are the shapes of the masses piled up in this region. Volcanic originally, the old craters are now fringed, where it is possible, with coral rocks which afford in only too many places no safe anchorage even for a boat. Merelava is an extinct volcano three thousand feet high, without a foot of level ground to all appearance. The steep incline plunges on all sides into the sea depths, and the *Southern Cross* has never found any spot where she can drop her anchor. Vanua Lava still smokes in places, the hot sulphurous steam telling of the fire that used to blaze, but is now extinguished. Rowa is a recent coral island almost level with the ocean surface; the shallow lagoons swarm with fish inside the barrier reef. Ureparapara presents a unique spectacle, for the old crater has broken out at one side, and the ship sails for a mile and a half into the heart of the mountain, finding no soundings until she has reached a little patch at the very end of this huge lake-like expanse. All around the precipitous sides, once a wall of scoria and lava, are now clothed from top to bottom with all the varied hues of tropical vegetation and gardens of cocoanuts and bananas. To the uninitiated eye, such slopes seem incapable of cultivation; but to the native they are his special delight for this purpose.

It is in such scenery as this that the Mission is doing its work. And it is the object of the following pages to take each island by itself, and to tell all that is known of its history and of the dawn of better days, when Christ's Gospel has banished the constant wars and murders which obtained of old, substituting the life hid with Christ in God; but, at the same time, interfering as little as possible with the customs of the natives.

THE ISLAND OF MOTA.

Seven schools; seven hundred and twenty baptized persons; one hundred and seventy-eight scholars; forty unbaptized; no heathens.

This island, though by no means the largest in

the group, merits the first place. No spot in the whole extent of the Mission has so settled a Christian life, and its language has virtually from the first been made the form of speech for mission teaching at Norfolk Island. I have inquired whether this action was taken after definite deliberation. But I am told that hardly so much as that can be alleged in its favour. Indeed, in the early days at St. John's College, Auckland, there was a short period during which a Solomon Island dialect was likely to be taken as the basis of communication. But in a short while Mota boys arrived in considerable numbers; their language commended itself by its richness in particles and prepositions, and gradually it established itself as worthy of the first place. Mota is really a volcano, long ago extinct, rising out of a plain of flat land round its base. Possibly a mile or two of level plain girdles the original hill, and I suspect that masses of coral reef, upraised in the course of centuries, are answerable for this level surface, carrying the old valcano with it in its upward trend. There is one great drawback to life here: there is no water except what may be found in holes in the coral, or saved after rain. It has been no uncommon thing for the clergyman in charge, whilst he has been staying here, to take the clothes that needed washing, and also every available cask and beaker, and transport himself in his boat to Vanua Lava, a distance of seven miles, in order to provide himself with clean garments and a sufficiency of pure liquid for his tea for the next few days to be spent at Mota. The natives, of course, subsist at such times on cocoanut milk; they can even drink brackish water; but neither of these have been found to brew good tea or coffee. To those who know the island as it is now it is hardly possible to credit the history of this spot thirty-five years ago.

In 1857 Bishop Selwyn took off from Port Patteson in Vanua Lava, seven miles off, two lads who ventured on board and were willing to stay. One of these was George Sarawia, a name known now to all who have heard of the Mission as the most faithful and consistent of all the native clergy. George, who was a Mota boy, relates how, when the sun went down that night, a great fear fell on him as he looked round the strange craft and unfamiliar faces. He thought his last hour was come. When evening prayers began he believed that after this religious ceremony he would be killed. He was down below and could not find his way up on deck: but the evening passed without mishap, and his doubts were dissipated. The next eight months he spent in New Zealand: then he returned to a school that had been started at Lifu. After this he remained under the care of Patteson, who helped to instil into him some of that sweetness of disposition which was his, and which is discernible in George—partly natural, and partly, I doubt not, the work of grace under the striking personality of his beloved master, the future bishop. It is strange to those who know George now, to hear that at this time for one season he went home, and was engaged in a fight and was wounded. He was the first baptized convert from the Banks Group, his baptism dating 1863. In 1865 he was confirmed and became a communicant. He was ordained deacon in 1868, and priest in 1873. He has always been the chief influence for good in Mota. His hair is now turning grey; no one who has met him can help calling him "dear George." His goodness and consistency appear in all he says and does.

It is not unfitting that I should dwell at some length on one who was the firstfruits of the Banks Islands, and a native of Mota. Bishop Selwyn says that on the day George came on board in 1857 he thought it advisable not to land as the people were so wild; but many swam out to the ship, and so they exchanged presents.

Five years passed, and in 1862 Bishop Patteson relates what the natives supposed him to be when he first landed. They knew he was not a man like themselves; he was the ghost of a man named Porisris come back to life again. This was clear, because as soon as Patteson had landed he walked into the house of the deceased man quite naturally. This belief that the white man is a ghost accounts for some of the attacks made upon the clergy in old days; for the natives fired their arrows, alleging that no such missiles could really injure a spirit returned from the unseen world. Soon after these days a school was formed at Mota on the same principle as one already mentioned at Lifu, and probably the choice of Mota was influenced by the fact that such a harbour as Port Patteson was so near. Scholars from other islands were brought here, and were cared for by Patteson, assisted by Dudley and Pritt, two of the early staff, in place of sailing all the way to New Zealand. Some of the boys had been trained partly in New Zealand; and Patteson relates how the heathen boys looked on in silent wonder whilst these maturer scholars cooked the food for all, washed up the utensils, and worked happily and methodically. Patteson says emphatically that these boys of his on this still savage island were acquiring insensibly the tone of a good English public school; they would of themselves put down lying, and stealing, and impurity. Thus the first island school took its rise. Yet the island was by no means full of Christians. No one stirred without bows and arrows. It was in these early days that a man used to say to Patteson, "May I walk with you to-day?" They accompanied him perhaps for two miles, and then confessed that they had never dared to travel so far before from their doors. On another occasion a boy lost his way entirely three-quarters of a mile from his home, for he had never left his village to go such a distance before. Patteson had noticed how, when a woman went a distance of a hundred and fifty yards to get water in a bamboo from a hole in the rock, her husband followed her with his bow and arrows, to cover her retreat in case she were attacked. Such details will not be thought unnecessary. They help us to bring vividly before our eyes the life of uncertainty and danger from which Christ's Gospel has freed these people for ever.

Have my readers ever attempted to realize the difficulty met with by those who have to speak of ideas common enough to our apprehension, but lying far outside the ken of a native's life?

The figure of God as a loving Shepherd—how can it be brought home to one who has seen no four-footed animal except a pig? How can the phrase "the Lamb of God," with all its profound lessons, be explained? Patteson gives us a forcible illustration of these difficulties by telling us that one day he began to teach a very able lad named Edmund Baratu, a native of Mota, the parables of the kingdom of heaven. He began to read the first words in the Gospel narrative—"The kingdom of heaven is like unto"—then it flashed upon him how little knowledge such a lad could possess of what a kingdom meant—a lad who knew no area larger than his little village. The bishop relates how it took him one and a half hours a day for a fortnight to explain the new ideas which were implied in a term which opened up so infinitely larger a conception of the world and of the unseen future, and its duties and ideals. It was not wasted time, let us be sure. It had far-reaching results, and established a basis for that higher teaching which revealed the world as potentially a great family—not at war, but living in peace and goodwill under the sheltering care of the Heavenly Father. Nine more years passed. It was now the beginning of 1871, a year never to be forgotten in the mission. Work had been steadily proceeding; and now a great awakening was at hand. Many in Mota said—so writes the bishop—" I see it all, and don't doubt it at all. I see that Jesus, whom the Father sent to be our Saviour, appointed baptism for the remission of sins, for gathering us into the body of the faithful. But it is so great a thing—it is so weighty that I fear lest I should break my promise, lest I should go back to my old ways." The bishop was there to give them comfort, and the early months of that year saw the baptism in Mota of two hundred and ninety-three persons—seventeen were boys from George Sarawia's school; forty-one were grown-up men and women; the rest were infants, whom the parents had promised to bring up as Christian children. We can see how God had sent this best of all encouragements to his servant, already worn with sickness, and prematurely old. The bishop knew not, however, how soon the call would come to summon him to lay down his task on earth. It was but a few weeks after he had seen the fruits of his labours at Mota, ere he met a martyr's death at the hands of men for whom, as the inscription upon his memorial cross says so well—" For whom he would have gladly given his life."

And what was the effect at Mota of the bishop's death? Consternation and doubt. They were among the first to hear the news. The vessel stood away from Nukapu for the Banks Islands, and not far from Mota, Joseph Atkin and Stephen Taroniara died of tetanus, and were committed to the deep.

Some said, now that the bishop was dead the Mission would come to an end. The boys that were at Norfolk Island would never return. At the peril of his life, George Sarawia went from island to island in the group, and explained that the work was God's work and that it would continue. When they threatened him with death, he said, "If you have any other reason for killing me, do so; but your boys are safe at Mota and at Norfolk Island."

The martyr death of the bishop had, indeed, the usual results. It strengthened, and did not in the end weaken the Church. That very year fifty-three more adults were baptized at Mota, and at a general muster of the schools in the island there were found to be three hundred and thirty-three scholars, with twenty-one teachers.

The history, however, of Christian life is never without its recurring trials for the faith of God's children. Hardly two years elapsed when, in 1873, disease swept through the island. In three months seventy baptized Christians died, and those who know natives best will realize how easily they suspect in these visitations the working of charms and spells. The deaths of those who were still heathens would quickly be laid at the doors of the Christians, and vengeance vowed against "the new teaching." Added to this, during the same year, or within a few months, a hurricane devastated the island and destroyed the crops and blew down the houses. It was a hard trial for the native deacon, George Sarawia. But he bore it well; and in the same year he was called to the priesthood, "having used the office of a deacon well, being found blameless."

Throughout these years, and indeed ever since, the Rev. J. Palmer was in charge of the schools in the Banks Group. He has many stories about his Mota people. At times he used to hold school in the open air. This had its advantages, but also its drawbacks. On one occasion he began his lesson thus, "I cannot begin, for I see some one smoking!" On another occasion he asked a child why he washed himself, expecting a very obvious answer; but the child replied, "To come to school." So Palmer ventured on another question. "I suppose you do not wash on Saturdays, then" (when there is no school)? "No," said the child, readily, and the answer was received with a burst of laughter from his companions.

The whole island is now Christian. George Sarawia does not lord it over his people, and therefore it comes to pass that he is sent for to compose quarrels, and is the valued adviser of all. In 1891 the Rev. T. G. Cullwick inaugurated a fresh advance in common, corporate life. On the festival of St. Philip and St. James there was a great meeting at the central place. The day began with a celebration of the Holy Communion, then followed the election of a sort of parliament of head men in each centre, and to this body were delegated powers for the benefit of the community. It is difficult to realize a greater change than such a scene presents from that state of things of which I have already spoken in 1857. In some thirty years the power of the Holy Spirit has transformed this island so that were the old inhabitants to rise from their graves they would not recognize their old homes. It is not because the people have been Anglicized, or made the slaves of the white man, or dress very differently, for they are unchanged in this, but because those who were once heathens are now Christians.

One of the teachers whom I met had a strange adventure with a shark at Mota. He was fishing in his canoe with his foot in the water. Suddenly a shark appeared, and pressed his nose against his foot. The boy sat still and with the point of his paddle gently pressed down the shark's head; but in a moment he re-appeared, and again began rubbing against the canoe apparently in a sportive vein. But the boy did not enjoy the fun; and by degrees he edged away, and finally slipped into the water at the approach of another canoe, and escaped in that, whilst the shark proceeded to tumble his old canoe over and over in play until it was broken to pieces.

I spent a very happy Sunday at Mota, holding a large confirmation in the open air. The altar was erected under a palm tree, and some four or five hundred people were present. I slept in the house built by the Rev. J. Palmer; and though the rats scampered about at night they did not nibble at my feet, though Mr. Palmer was not so fortunate. I shall not easily forget the merry dances of the children on the Saturday evening in the moonlight, singing songs the while; and I wish the tunes could have been taken down, for they were full of beauty, whilst they differed in character from English music. On all sides there was friendliness. On one occasion, as I was standing conversing with some of the people (through an interpreter), I received a message to ask if I would walk over to a group of men who had come from the other end of the island for, so the message ran, "they wish to look at you." I gladly obeyed, and I trust I was able to contribute to their amusement and edification. A few weeks afterwards, on the return of the *Southern Cross* from the north, I spent another night here; and on this occasion I was fortunate enough to see a sight of which I had heard much, but never hoped to behold. At nine o'clock in the evening, George Sarawia came to say, "They expect the *Un* to come in to-morrow morning at about three o'clock, when the moon is above the trees." Let me explain for the benefit of my readers that I was about to witness one of the most curious phenomena in nature, at least so it seems to be in my opinion. In the South Seas, along the coral reefs, there appears on certain special occasions a sort of sea worm which is born in the interstices of the coral. It is a long thread-like thing, sometimes a foot in length, white in colour, and so thin that it often breaks in the hands when lifted up. These creatures make their appearance on only two or three occasions in the year. These visits can be calculated with great exactness; they come at a certain phase of the moon, and at night; a month elapses, and again they appear at the same time, to the very day and hour. This happens on only three nights in the year, and in the Banks Group it is during October or November.

At two a.m. we were stumbling over rough coral in the bush; the coral was strewn with leaves and rendered invisible thereby, a most painful sort of roadway. By the help of a lantern we made our way to the shore, from which already shouts were heard in all directions.

Far along to right and left lights were twinkling along the reefs; these were torches made of dry brushwood, which burnt with great brillancy, and lighted up the waves as they broke upon the shore. We hurried up to a group of men and women, who were standing up to their knees in water lining the sides of the deep channels in the coral reef. These channels are in themselves full of interest; often not more than five or six feet wide, they are as much as ten and twelve feet deep, and transparently clear, so that one feels as if it were a precipice more than a channel of water. As the fishers waved their torches and held them up over their heads we could see that the water was full of myriads of long thread-like creatures, twisting and turning in all directions and carried backwards and forwards in the wash of the waves. Some men had large flat nets made of a sort of rough muslin, with which they skimmed off hundreds of the worms, and transferred them to pots; others simply dipped their hands among these creatures and took them out. Now and again they would burst into a native song, which would be taken up by the others, and the sound would float away until it mingled with the voices of others who were plying their strange task further along these shores. I was given to understand that the same scene was being enacted on all the shores of the Banks Islands on this night. When daylight comes these coral worms vanish, nor do they appear again for a month, returning with such regularity when the moon is right for them that it seems as if I were telling a fairy tale, rather than recounting an actual adventure. Under the name of "Balolo" the "un" is known well in Fiji, and, I suppose, in all the coral islands of these seas. I ought to have mentioned that in walking quickly along the sandy beach we had passed what looked like a number of mats thrown carelessly about. In reality these were the coverings drawn over men and women and children, who were asleep in the holes which they had made in the sand. The whole population seemed to have streamed down to the shore to aid in this strange annual harvest of worms, and though the mats were lying level with the ground, the appearance of a toe here and there peeping out at one corner revealed the fact of sleeping occupants, and fortunately prevented us from treading upon our friends, who were sleeping the sleep of the just. We returned in due time to our beds, and in the morning at breakfast time I gave one of the most signal proofs of courage that I can remember. I asked if I might taste the "un" caught that morning. I asked thoughtlessly, and in a short time a little green bundle of leaves was brought in. I opened it, and saw inside what looked like a little heap of green lobworms. It was too late to retract; my honour was at stake. Therefore, closing my eyes, I boldly took a mouthful and swallowed it. The taste was not unpleasant, resembling shell-fish in the shape of vermicelli.

I may mention here that one of the regular signs of Christian life, and one of the most delightful to contemplate, is the daily gathering of the whole community for their morning and evening prayer in their church. At about seven a.m. the church is filled; each man and woman kneels on entering; nor during the service is such a thing so much as heard of that any one should sit during prayer. A hymn is sung, together with one of the canticles; one of the daily lessons is read, and a shortened form of daily prayer is said by the clergyman or teacher in charge. The same obtains at about seven o'clock every evening. Such a custom is universal among all the hundreds of schools in Melanesia, carrying out the Church's rule of daily prayer in a manner which would astonish many of our own church people who have never known such a rule for themselves. Every custom has, of course, its dangers. I imagine that such regular united worship twice a day may easily check in some cases the spontaneous outpouring of the soul in individual private devotion. But this tendency is well known, and can be counteracted. No one can fail to be touched and to be deeply thankful to hear, as one sails along the shores of one of these islands, say, at sunset, the call to prayer in some village hidden among the cocoanuts; it may be the tinkling of a small bell, or the boom of a native conch shell, or the beat of a drum made out of a hollowed-out tree. It proclaims that family prayer is about to begin, and that the Heavenly Father is not so forgotten ere the people retire to slumber. The number of the baptized at Mota at this time is seven hundred and seventy. The actual scholars in school are one hundred and seventy-eight. There are but thirty left who are as yet unbaptized in Mota. It should be stated also that holy baptism is preceded by a most careful examination; at the service itself each adult candidate answers each of the four questions singly by himself, no matter how great the numbers are. With regard to Mota, be it recorded to its honour, the people have always been ready to go out in the true missionary spirit as teachers to other islands. At the present time there are thirteen Mota teachers engaged in other islands, some of them as far away as the Solomons.

CHAPTER VI.

THE ISLAND OF SANTA MARIA.

WELVE schools; six hundred and forty-four baptized Christians; two hundred and twenty-six scholars in school; one thousand and sixty-seven attending services; one thousand seven hundred heathens.

Santa Maria is one of the largest of the Banks Group, sharing the distinction of size with Vanua Lava. Its name suggests, what is the fact, that the Spaniards named it at the same time that they discovered and named Spiritu Santo, one of the Hebrides, which adjoins it. It is some twelve miles in length, and at the northern end there are two volcanic peaks about six miles apart. Between these two summits there is now a large and deep lake, which is supposed to be the ancient crater, or, perhaps, it may be two craters burst into one vast chasm.

The larger islands in Melanesia have been, as a rule, the most difficult for the mission. The four of the Banks Group, which are entirely Christian, are among the four smallest, but on Santa Maria there are still one thousand seven hundred heathens. Thirty years ago the mission gained a hold on this island by obtaining a few boys for instruction; these have now become five hundred, and these figures may be more than doubled if all who attend the services, and are soon to be baptized, are taken into account, and let it be remembered that this work has been done principally by native Christians themselves; this is the glory of the Mission. Having reached one of the larger islands, it is fitting to call attention, at once, to the difficulties which beset Mission work in such places. The superintending clergyman is acquainted with the whole island, and, therefore, it is possible to give accurate statistics. But his difficulty is connected with the language. It is hard for English people to realize that the natives live in such an isolated manner in their villages that a dialect spoken in one village is unintelligible in another two miles off. They are of course dialects, but so diverse that they are practically a bar to communication. Santa Maria has three distinct districts marked by differences of speech and manners. On the north-east Gaua, on the west Lakona, and Koro on the south. Lakona is the best known to traders and labour vessels, because there is a watering-place on this side; and it is common to hear them speak of the island of Lakona. To the mission the east coast is the most inaccessible. It feels the full force of the trade wind, and hardly presents any anchorage or harbour, even for a whaleboat. It is a most serious drawback, and it is not surprising that this is the side where schools are most difficult to plant. Of course the elder Selwyn landed on Santa Maria. I do not find that he ever passed any of these islands without going ashore. It must have been about 1855, that he was at Lakona where there is now a flourishing school. Just to the north of the landing-place there is a rock jutting out into the sea, called now "Cock Sparrow Point." The Spaniards tell us that from this point they were fired at by the natives, and it is remarkable that they treated Selwyn in the same manner from the same spot. He had succeeded in landing safely lower down, but, on returning, the young sparks had rushed on ahead, burning to kill the intruders.

In the same year, Bishop Selwyn landed at Gaua (on the north-east) for the first time, and was met by an excited crowd of natives, all armed, who rushed down to meet the white man. Selwyn took a bow out of a man's hand and drew with it a line upon the sand, and explained by signs that he and they should severally keep upon opposite sides of it. Those who were present say that by the innate dignity of his presence, and his calm and courteous bearing, he entirely succeeded in his overcoming their suspicions. Patteson, who was present, gave a fish-hook to one of the natives. Years afterwards Marauvelav, a teacher, told the future bishop that it was he who had received the present.

There are no natives in the group so quarrelsome as the Santa Maria folk, especially at Gaua, the eastern section. Murders have been very common here. As I was standing on the beach at Gaua I was told how Baratu, one of our teachers, was an eye-witness, on that very spot, of a death under peculiarly distressing circumstances. A man a little way inland had killed another. The relatives of the murdered man, of course, vowed vengeance, but as they were unable to capture the actual offender they determined to attack some relative. Just after this a brother of the offender returned from Brisbane, where he had been labouring for some time, and was, of course, absolutely ignorant of what had happened at Gaua. He had just landed and was standing on the beach beside his box, Baratu being close to him, when the latter heard some one say, "Stand firm." Instantly there was a report of a gun, and the poor returned labourer fell dead where he had been standing. Shocking as these cases are, much as they remind us of the death of Bishop Patteson, let us at least remember that for these poor savages there is no regular court of justice. The only reparation possible is that which is enforced by private individuals, and "an eye for an eye" is the rule. The people at Lakona, on the western side, seem to be as fond of a fight as the proverbial Irishman. On such occasions they go to work systematically, and mark out a definite fighting ground; sometimes they will break off by consent and arrange to begin again on a specified day. What is still more curious, is that when such a battle is announced the young men of a neighbouring village, who have nothing to do with the quarrel, will take their bows and arrows and start off to take part in the conflict. Strangest of all, is the fact that such a party, who go from sheer love of fighting, usually divide into two parties and choose to oppose each other. The division is made by the two sides of the house according to the native marriage laws, both sides being always of necessity represented in every village; and an explanation of this custom will be given in another place. If one of these light-hearted warriors kills one of his own people he never returns again to his village.

It may be of interest also to describe a method of dunning unwilling debtors at Lakona: civilized nations might well take a hint and adopt the same process. If payment cannot be obtained from a man, the people who are interested make up a party and quietly encircle the debtor's house at night, sleeping all round it. In the morning they commence living upon the man's substance, and they continue to billet themselves upon him till he pays the debt. The food consumed during these raids is not considered in the payment of the sum owed. I am told also that here when a man borrows a sum of money he pays the interest beforehand, and it is conceivable that he may be unable to borrow altogether if he has not sufficient to pay the interest before anything is entrusted to him.

When I landed at Lakona the boat was still in the water, and a man came forward and offered to carry me ashore. I discovered afterwards that this individual was an interesting character. The people of Lakona and Koro had a fight a few years ago: the man I allude to, a native of Koro, happened to kill a Lakona man. The Lakona men sent a message to Koro to say that there were only two courses open to the individual who had taken their friend's life. He would either be killed in revenge some day, however long they might have to wait; or else he might, if he chose, come over to them, give up Koro, and become a Lakona man, taking the place of the deceased, marrying his wife, adopting his children, and accepting his property. Accordingly, knowing that there was really no alternative, he came and took up all the privileges of his opponent, and I saw him happy and contented on the day of which I speak. The death of the fortunate might in our day become too common if the murderer were always rewarded with the goods of his victim.

There is one native custom which has to some degree held its own since the introduction of the "New Teaching." Dr. Codrington says: "It was a matter of principle with Bishop Patteson not to interfere in an arbitrary manner with the institutions of the people, but to leave it to their own sense of right and wrong, and their own knowledge of the character of what they did, to condemn or to tolerate what their growing enlightenment would call in question. So there arose among his early pupils the doubt whether it would be right for them as Christians to continue members of the 'Tamate' societies, to seek admission into them, and frequent their lodges. The bishop put it to them that they should inquire and consult among themselves about the real character of the societies: Did they offer worship and prayer to ghosts and spirits? Were they required to take part in anything indecent or atrocious? Did membership involve any profession of belief or practice of superstition peculiar to the members? After consultation, they reported to him that they could not discover anything wrong in itself, except the pretence of association with ghosts which had already ceased to be serious, and the beating and robbing of the uninitiated, which it was quite possible for them to refuse to take part in and to oppose. The bishop, therefore, would not condemn the societies." This extract is given to show the principles of the Mission in such matters. The "Tamate" is the secret society which exists in some form in many groups of these islands. No women or children are ever permitted to be initiated, or to watch any of the details of its working. The members dress up in grotesque headpieces, and in a kind of petticoat of banana fibre. They have their house, which is approached by paths, guarded with signs denoting that none but members may approach. From time to time uncouth figures, clad in masks, issue forth and dance, and sometimes beat and rob those they meet. The house of the Tamate is called the Salagoro. Here persons are initiated, and sometimes they are compelled to remain within the house for periods varying from six to a hundred days. In the absence of people with authority in these islands, such a secret society has a salutary effect. For instance, one day a man had been wounded; next morning the cry went forth that the Tamate were out. The society had made it a rule that bows and fighting arrows were not to be used, following the teaching of Bishop Patteson. Thus a rude justice was maintained, which would seem impossible otherwise, for in the Banks Group there never have been chiefs who are invested with any real power. A boy is at an early age independent of all authority, and protects himself with his own bow and arrow. The Salagoro of the Tamate is used as a kind of club house for the members. Here they can live if they choose, and cook their food and pass their time. Of late it appears that these rites have injured the schools by the length of time over which they extend. A meeting of the Christians was held in order so to modify their customs as to make them innocent. I believe the course proposed by the teachers was adopted readily.

The schools in Santa Maria now number twelve. They are pretty evenly distributed, except upon the eastern side. Here the coral reef presents no boat harbour, and the trade wind brings a heavy surf up. The people, however, have asked for a teacher, which means that they definitely desire to become Christians. On the north-east shore of this island there is a barrier reef, through which there is a channel with a safe anchorage inside it. It is always a treat to watch the captain of the *Southern Cross* bringing his vessel to anchorage here and taking her out. It requires considerable skill, but it is always effected with ease. I have already mentioned feats of swimming on the part of natives; here is another story. A story is told of a woman of Mota, who was displeased with the treatment she received from her husband; she took to the sea and probably intended reaching Vanua Lava, which is only seven miles off, and has often been reached by persecuted wives. But in this case the tide drifted the woman away, helped by a strong sea breeze, and she landed on Santa Maria near Lakona, having accomplished a distance of twenty miles. She took up her residence at Lakona, and her descendants record her exploit to this day. On the morning that I landed at Lakona, there was to be a solemn service of baptism. Some twenty-six adults were baptized by the Rev. T. C. Cullwick. The church was crowded, and afterwards the enclosure in front of the building was filled with picturesque groups of Christians, whilst from the little plateau where the church and school stand, lovely views are to be obtained over the bay and forest clad cliffs, and the blue sea beyond. At Koro we visited the school, and there met Baratu, whose name has already been mentioned. The next day we entered the reef at Gaua and visited the north-eastern schools. Some weeks afterwards we were off these shores again and watered the ship at "Black Beach;" the scene is depicted in one of the best photographs we took during the tour. Several of the clergy have made expeditions to the lake on the plateau, near the old volcanic peaks, and when I come to discourse upon the doings of the mythical personage named Qat, the lake in question will take a prominent place in the story of that remarkable individual. The waters of the lake discharge themselves into the sea by a magnificent waterfall. I think it will be granted that such an island is a field in itself for a white clergyman. But it is only one of a large group under one white member of the Mission. It is a heavy responsibility, and indeed there is not one of these workers who does not need our earnest prayers for health and strength and zeal to break down all barriers and bring all under the yoke of Christ.

MERELAVA (or STAR ISLAND).

Five schools; two hundred and five baptized persons; eighty-four scholars; four hundred and ninety-four listeners; two hundred heathens. The Rev. William Vaget, a deacon, is in charge.

For strangeness of form, Merelava and Ureparapara divide the honours in this Banks Group of islands. No one who has sailed close by these two places is ever likely to forget them. Merelava is the most southern of the group, and not more than twenty miles from Aurora, the most northern of the New Hebrides. On the occasion when I first approached it, I had been busy writing in the cabin, and had not observed that we were approaching this old volcano. On coming on deck I found myself within a couple of miles of one of the most striking objects I have ever witnessed. Before my eyes there towered a precipitous mass, sloping sharply up to a height of three thousand feet, straight from the sea level. There appeared to be not a single yard of level ground. There was no break in the precipitous ascent up to the summit. The whole of this vast mass was coated with the greenest of vegetation up to the old crater. Just a patch of bare earth (scoria and lava) was visible

Archdeacon Palmer at Merelava.

up in the clouds. I had no time to ascend to the top, but I am informed that a deep crater with perpendicular walls on one side still exists; or rather there is a crater within a crater, the inner one being complete in shape. It is the habit of boys to run races round this vast basin.

The ship gradually approached the mountain, and then I discovered that there was no anchorage whatever. The steep slope of the hill is apparently continued under the surface of the sea. At any rate, there are no practicable soundings anywhere, and the ship hangs on and off till the boat returns. An old lava stream, stiffened into a mass of sharp edges and contorted seams, serves as a landing-stage. And on this dark ledge, reminding me of the general shape of the Giants' Causeway in Ireland (though one is mere lava, and the other crystallized basalt), the greater part of the population usually assembles, clad in bright colours, so far as they are clad at all. It forms a beautiful picture in the tropical sunlight, framed in blue sea on one side, and green forest on the other. It is all the more pleasant to visit Merelava, because the people are so warm-hearted and affectionate. They have ever borne this character, and the work of the Mission is bright with hope for the future. I have not mentioned before that on every island in these parts there are returned labourers.. I learnt that from this mere speck in the ocean, for instance, there were at the time of my landing fifty-five labourers absent, chiefly working in Fiji. I met many who could talk English, and a friend who could talk Fijian found no difficulty in discoursing with a great many of the people. One idea may safely be banished for ever, namely, that these islanders do not understand what the labour traffic means. I have no hesitation in saying that every one understands all that it means. But the subject of the labour traffic demands an article to itself, and I return to the history of Merelava. The first boys were taken to Kohimarama about the year 1864. In 1866, when the settlement at Norfolk Island was commenced, a pair of twins were among those who were permitted to leave Merelava, and were among the first who settled in the new Mission school. But in 1867, just a year after the happy opening of the new venture in that lovely paradise of the southern ocean, typhoid fever broke out in the Mission. I believe the disease was traced without any doubt to the Norfolk Islanders. During the course of the fever these twins from Merelava both died. They had endeared themselves to all who knew them, and great was the sorrow when it pleased God to take them to Himself. The news had to be carried to their island home. When it had been told, a younger brother in the same family, Marau by name, jumped into the boat, seated himself by the bishop, took his hand and could not be induced to leave him. The uncle of the boy, grieved at the death of the two others, and believing that the bishop had made the first move in desiring to take away another member of the same family, became very angry, and would have attacked the boat, possibly with very serious consequences, had not the rest of the people, seeing how matters were, and perceiving that it was the boy's own expressed wish, held back the infuriated relative. Marau was brought to Norfolk Island. In due time he was baptized as Clement, and at this time he is known as the Rev. Clement Marau, the ablest of all the native clergy, a beautiful musician, playing both upon the organ and the violin. Clement also has shown the true missionary spirit. He has gone to Ulaua in the Solomon Islands, there we shall hear of him again.

But the first school on Merelava was begun by those willing teachers, the natives of Mota and Motlav. They continued the work until a boy named William Vaget returned from Norfolk Island. It was my privilege to ordain William Vaget a deacon at Norfolk Island in the Mission Chapel, and to bring him to Merelava and introduce him to his own people as their first ordained clergyman; and afterwards I returned, after an absence of a few weeks, and confirmed ten of his people. There are now five schools on the island; two hundred and five people are baptized; the schools contain eighty-four young scholars, though the total of those who are under some amount of instruction is four hundred and ninety-four. There are, however, still about two hundred heathens. But I believe these will soon be won to acknowledge the Father of our Lord Jesus Christ as their God and Lord. There has always existed a kindly spirit among these people. We are told that some forty years ago a whaleboat, with a crew of five men, landed here, and on this still heathen island they were kindly received, and were eventually taken off by another ship.

The school village where William Vaget lives is reached by a lovely path which ascends through glades of forest trees and palms until the visitor is landed on a small flat spot dug out of the mountain. The prospect is magnificent, overlooking the sea with the islands of this group and of the Hebrides dotted over its surface. The gardens of the natives, steep enough in most islands, seem here to be almost perpendicular against the sides of this magnificent old volcano. I have written this, feeling that there is a romance about this spot which appeals strongly to my feelings; and I should be glad if my words have helped the friends of the Mission to realize this particular centre of our work. Merelava is indeed a worthy warder standing guard over the Banks Island as the mission ship sails north after leaving the New Hebrides. It is remarkable that the northernmost point of the same group should be another solitary volcano even more remarkable, namely, Ureparapara. Some weeks afterwards, when I was passing a few hours on a labour vessel in Vila Harbour, in the New Hebrides, I met several Merelava men and one or two women also. They were perfectly happy, having engaged themselves with a complete knowledge of the work that was expected of them. The ship was taking them to Queensland, though as a rule the Merelava people have chosen Fiji as their usual wage-earning centre. The ship had come into port in search of a doctor, for the Government agent had been stabbed by one of the labourers. Of course the first thought was that it was a case of revenge upon one who had been kidnapping an unsuspecting man. But it was nothing of the kind. The man was mad; and after handing the agent two pounds to keep for him, he drew his knife and struck him. The rest of the labourers were so indignant that it was with difficulty they were prevented from throwing him at once into the sea. Nothing could have been happier than the relations between the captain and the agent and all who were on board.

THE ISLAND OF MERIG.

One school; sixteen baptized persons; twenty-two scholars.; thirty-six Church attendants; no heathens.

Merig is a miniature Mota. Indeed, if report says true, a former captain of the *Southern Cross* once insisted that Merig was not itself but Mota, and was much confounded when he discovered his error. It is needless to say that the present captain of the Mission ship is incapable of such a mistake. But it is a fact that Merig is a miniature Mota. It has the same sort of extinct volcano as a centre; then, in place of exhibiting precipitous slopes descending into the sea, such as at Merelava, it has a fair margin of level land on all sides, probably a coral reef raised gradually in the course of centuries. I suppose the entire length of the island cannot be more than a mile and a half. When the ship is some ten miles distant, Merelava and Merig present a strange contrast (they are only separated by about twelve miles of water). Merelava towers into the sky like a huge monster, visible for sixty miles on each side. Merig at even ten miles distance shows none of its flat land, and looks like a solitary point of rock set up by itself in the ocean. There is no more inaccessible spot than this little island. There is nothing approaching even to a boat harbour. All around, the coral ridges descend steep into the sea and the surf thunders perpetually on them as the trade wind and current drive past this islet on to the shores of Santa Maria westward. There is hardly a spot where the clergyman's whale boat can be drawn up for the night. It is but rarely, therefore, that he can pay a visit here of more than a few hours' duration. To anchor a boat in deep water off such reefs as these, causes so much anxiety to the owner when he ought to be asleep, that it is hardly a practicable suggestion. Often no attempt can be made to effect a landing, even on the lee side. In such cases the people do not hesitate to jump off their rocks and to swim out to the boat ; and it is a merry and amusing scene to converse with people perfectly at home in the water who bring yams for sale, and ask for gifts in return. The first teaching ever given here, was through the instrumentality of a returned labourer. It was about the year 1886, that he swam off to the boat, and asked if he could have a book with which to teach the people to read. Cards, with letters of the alphabet, and a few books, were given him, and holding them over his head he swam back in triumph and commenced his school. I am glad to be able to record here the willingness of a returned labourer to help his people in the best of ways. It is no uncommon thing ; a good many of them are teachers under the Mission ; and the majority of them, in many islands, take their places among their fellows again and attend school with the rest, and are indistinguishable from the others, except that they know a few words of English. They bear a good character and appear not to have been injured by their residence in Queensland or Fiji. It is remarkable indeed that in such an inaccessible spot as Merig the labour traffic should be thoroughly understood. I met several on shore at this place, when I had the good fortune to effect a landing. The boat was brought up to the reef, which presented its usual precipitous descent into the surf. The swell rose and fell, at one moment raising the boat high above the edge, whilst the waves broke in foam over the coast ; but the next moment the boat had fallen several feet below the ridge. Watching our opportunity, we had to jump from the boat whilst a native kept the bow from grounding on the reef ; and no worse fate attended us than wet trousers up to the knees, and a most slippery walk over the submerged coral. Just at the usual landing-stage there is a curious crevice in the coral rock, which sobs and sighs as the wind from a cavern below rushes up through it. The natives pour mud into it in order to see it blown away, when a wave below forces the air upward. In days gone by the Mission folk discovered that there were only eighteen persons living on the Merig, and these eighteen were at enmity and not on speaking terms! This state of things has passed away. The whole island is now under Christian influences. A teacher and his wife, both from Merelava, are doing a good work. Sixteen persons are as yet baptized; there are twenty-two young scholars in the school, and the whole of the thirty-six people who live on Merig are at present under instruction.

CHAPTER VII.

THE ISLAND OF VANUA LAVA.

EIGHT schools; three hundred and fifty-one baptized; one hundred and thirty-four scholars; five hundred and sixty-eight attending services; five hundred and twenty heathens.

The centre of the main group of these islands is Vanua Lava, meaning "large land." It presents a beautiful spectacle from almost any point of view. There are fantastic shaped mountains with precipitous sides, the relics of extinct volcanoes—and still at one point the vapours from sulphur springs are seen rising like white clouds from the slope of one of these hills.

On the eastern shore lies Port Patteson, named in early days by Selwyn and Patteson after Judge Patteson, the noble father of the bishop. It is a safe harbour at any time, a rare thing in this group. It may almost be said to be the only harbour in the Banks Islands. The *Southern Cross* usually anchors here for a few nights whilst the clergy are visiting Mota and Motlav. It is not a healthy place. Mangrove swamps taint the air and suggest fever. A river runs into the harbour, named Crocodile River. But, strange to say, no crocodile had ever been heard of here until the trip of 1892. A dark object was seen by a boat manned by Solomon Islanders and others who are familiar with the saurians; and they all exclaimed, "There is a crocodile!" without being aware that the river was so named.

It is a great place for crayfish. Seventy were brought to the ship one day, and before evening they had all been devoured, so large is the company on board, and so welcome is this dainty to Melanesians and English alike. The schools on this island are seven in number at present; but as for the people themselves they do not seem very capable. Indeed it is a remarkable fact, that nearly all the teachers in the Vanua Lava schools, are at this time either Mota, or Motlav men. One amongst these stands pre-eminent for the good work he did, Edwin Sakelrau, and his wife Emma —both are dead now; but it will be long ere their names are forgotten. They came from Motlav to Pek in 1878, on the northern shore, and found the people living inland in somewhat inaccessible places. They discovered a healthy site on a rising ground overlooking the sea, and well watered by rushing streams. Here they built their school, and gradually induced their people to come and settle round them, till quite a little community of Christians was formed here. On one Sunday evening I confirmed thirty-five of their number. Edwin Sakelrau was the brother of Henry Tagalana, the latter being the head native clergyman at Motlav. Edwin, his brother, was ordained a deacon in 1878 by Bishop Selwyn, at Ra, an island adjoining Motlav. The *Southern Cross* brought over for that occasion many Christians from Pek, where Edwin was working, a distance of some ten miles. Bishop Selwyn writes: "We brought out the little altar table and set it up under the overhanging eaves of the schoolhouse, and made a rude rail. The ground sloped away, and in the background was a magnificent banian tree. . . . I am sure no bishop ever sent forth a more simple, earnest man to do His Master's work. And I am very happy about him." Five years afterwards, in 1883, Edwin died at Pek. His wife followed him, only too soon for the people of the place; for she was a great power for good at Pek. The reason the inhabitants had left the seashore was that they had been decimated by dysentery in the spot which they had chosen for their village. But Edwin induced them to return to a most healthy spot at Pek. From a kind of natural terrace, upon which the church and the houses stand, there is a lovely outlook through the trees across the sea with Ureparapara in the distance, with its remarkable crater open to the sea.

Many have left this island in labour vessels. This indeed is true of every spot in these parts, and though it is natural that Christian teachers should regret the departure often of their best scholars, yet it is a not unnatural result of the opening of the eyes of the people by Christian teaching. They hear for the first time of the great world beyond, and they are seized with a longing to go and see it for themselves. It is better to prepare them for the dangers they may encounter than to be silent on such a topic, and stand unwisely in their way.

Vanua Lava was touched by Bishop Selwyn in 1857. It was then that George Sarawia was taken up in Port Patteson. The story of his sensations at the time, and of his after career, is given in the account of the island of Mota. During his second landing in Vanua Lava the bishop proceeded to buy yams by weight. A steelyard was attached to a stout branch, and money was paid according to the scale. It is said that the natives were delighted at the justice of the proceeding. When at times yams were taken off the scale because they weighed too heavily for the sum offered, there was a hum of approval, and probably nothing was so great a help to the cause of the Mission than such an exhibition of even-handed justice.

There are of course incidents to be related which the people tell with amusement. A short while ago Benjamin Virsal, the teacher at Vureas, on the western side of this island, swallowed a fish bone, which, however, stuck in his throat. Nothing the people could do appeared of the slightest use; the bone was refractory and kept its place, and poor Benjamin was unable to eat, and became a shadow of his former self. His friends thought he would die, and they put him in a canoe to convey him to Mota that he might be buried among his own people. There is a very strong tide which runs round a well-known point on the way to Mota, and soon the canoe was dancing over the waves, and was giving the occupants of it a rare shaking. To the astonishment and delight of the rowers a great jolt at last dislodged the bone, and it fell out. Benjamin soon recovered, and is now well and at work in his old school.

The neighbourhood of Vureas seems to be favourable to strange experiences, for on another occasion a woman here was placing her hand in a hole to draw something out. In order to do this she had to lie down and put her arm into the place as far as it could be made to go. At this critical moment her fingers were seized by a large crab who would not relax his hold. The woman no doubt struggled and shouted, but no one heard her cries. There she lay for part of a day and all the next night, until she was found by some children who hurried home with the news. Her husband soon appeared and dragged her arm out and also the crab, very quickly.

There are seven schools at the present time in Vanua Lava; I visited three of them, and held two confirmations. The baptized number three hundred and fifty-seven; the young scholars are one hundred and thirty-four; the total number, including all who are listeners, is five hundred and sixty-eight; and there are five hundred and twenty who are still heathens in a full sense. Here, as in Santa Maria (these being the largest islands), it has been difficult to win the people as quickly as in smaller islands.

For the sake of those who are interested in the most characteristic customs of the Melanesians, and wish to understand their manner of life, I will give here the substance of a chapter in Dr. Codrington's book on Melanesian folk lore. The custom to which I allude is called the Suqe; it has not receded before Christianity. There is no particular reason indeed why it should on this island, for there is nothing bad about it; and I had many opportunities of watching its action.

"In every village, and group of houses in the Torres Islands, the Banks Islands, and the northern New Hebrides, is conspicuous a building which does not appear to be a dwelling-house. In a populous village of the Banks Islands it is very long and low, with entrances at intervals along the sides below the wall-plate, with stone seats or a stone platform at the main entrances at either end, and low stone walls planted with dracænas and crotons, with the jawbones of pigs and backbones of fish hanging under the eaves; and very often the clatter of sticks pounding in wooden vessels, and the presence of white clouds of steam make known the preparation of a meal. This place is a 'Gamal.' It is virtually a club-house for men. Women are not admitted into it nor young children. Virtually all the male population have in their day been initiated and have paid their fees to win the right of a place in it. If there is any one who has no place in the gamal, he is nicknamed after a kind of flying fox, which is in the habit of living a solitary life. I have been often struck by the immense length of these long houses, extending sometimes for forty yards and more. There is nothing secret about them, for they are often the most conspicuous object in the village. Were you to enter one of them, you would notice at once certain log boundaries which separate a number of ovens from each other. And round the ovens are mats and cooking utensils. The general name for such a club in the Banks Islands—at Vanua Lava, as much as elsewhere—is 'Suqe.'"

These ovens represent different gradations in rank. Each step for permission to use another oven in a higher place has to be paid for by heavy fees; and no one can have any great authority in his village who has not risen high in the Suqe. I gather that the highest rank of all is rarely reached. When a man has attained this exalted position he is a very great personage; and his permission would have to be obtained before any one could be advanced at all to any grade. The number of ovens in a complete Suqe is eighteen; it will easily be imagined how heavy must be the tax upon a man's resources if he wishes to reach the topmost step. I used to notice that sometimes one end of the gamal looked new, as if it had been recently added to. The reason, probably, was that some one had risen to a higher grade, and had built himself a new oven above the others. Sometimes, also, one end of the gamal was in ruins. This probably meant that there was no one to use the ovens at that end, and it was no one's business to keep the structure in that spot in repair. As a rule, the most of the men never rise above middle rank, but most of them are initiated when they are boys. If a gamal only possesses five or six ovens it means that there is no one in the village who has attained a higher rank. It is needless to add that no one would dare to use an oven of a rank above his own. He would meet with instant and severe punishment. If a stranger comes to a village he is entertained in the gamal and sleeps there. He is made, in fact, an honorary member of the local club. I gather that in Mota the lowest grade can be reached by the payment of half a fathom of native shell money; but as the grades rise money sometimes fails, and pigs, which are expensive creatures, are brought into requisition. Perhaps there is no better way of showing the position that the Suqe holds in the imagination of the people than to record that in native stories where the fortunes of an orphan boy are related, who wins his way to fame, it is by the gradations of the Suqe that he makes his progress in life. It is manifest that such a social institution as this which I have described is of use in preserving and maintaining order in a native community.

Perhaps nothing will show the difficulty of mission work in an island such as Vana Lava so much as the fact that in this small space, not more than twelve miles by ten, there are sixteen dialects, many of them very different from each other. Such difficulties help us to understand why a large island holds out longer against the work of the Mission than one of a smaller area, where there is not this confusion of tongues. I twice visited Vanua Lava. It is generally easy to land, because Pek, the most important station, is on the lee side, and Port Patteson, a safe harbour, is at the other extremity. Between these on the west side is Vureas. It is a beautiful spot, with hills towering above the ship, but it is one of the gustiest anchorages I ever experienced. The captain of a sailing vessel has to keep a very sharp look-out, for the squalls rush down first on one quarter, then on the other, without any warning, and it is easy to lose control of the ship. The fact is, Vureas is in an eddy of the sea breeze, and the surface of the little bay is continually being whitened by these sudden gusts. It was here that I met my friend who had swallowed the fish bone, and had been so mercifully assisted by the tide rip. Here also, on Vanua Lava, is the mountain of Qat, whose story will be told under the head of the Island of Motlav.

It was at Pek that I had, perhaps, the most delightful bathe in the whole tour. We undressed, I remember, in a hut about half a mile from the stream, as it was raining. Then we ran, with shouts, a merry party, black and white, through the wood till we stood over a deep stream bursting into a hole after a plunge of a good many feet. Into this hole we also plunged, black and white together. I remember the merry scamper back to the hut, and the delight at the coffee which was ready for us there. I have reasons, both grave and gay, for remembering Pek, in Vanua Lava.

THE ISLAND OF UREPARAPARA, OR BLIGH ISLAND.

Two schools; one hundred and fifty-three baptized; sixty-seven scholars; one hundred and eighty-eight attending services; one hundred and eighty heathens.

Just as Merelava, a cone three thousand feet in height and plunging straight into the sea, is the sentinel of the Banks Islands to the visitor from the south, so Ureparapara, with its still more striking configuration, is the most northern outpost. Close past this spot, Captain Bligh passed during the most wonderful boat voyage that has ever been successfully made, after the mutiny of the *Bounty* in Tahiti. After the brave navigator, it has been called Bligh Island. But the Mission always uses the native name, which is to my ears more appropriate to its romantic interest—Ureparapara. It is a vast volcano, not so lofty as Merelava, but extending a great distance horizontally. When it was in a state of eruption in past ages, it must have presented an appalling prospect, for the crater is fully two miles in length, by some mile or so in breadth from edge to edge. The eastern end of this enormous crater has been completely blown away. There is apparently no ridge or bar except at some unknown depth; but the sea rolls in with unruffled surface, and the *Southern Cross* has found no soundings in this deep gulf till the very innermost edge is reached at the western end of the crater.

It is a sight not to be forgotten when the ship takes a sharp turn, and steams straight into the heart of the mountain. The deep water at the entrance is fully half a mile in width. Before the spectator there lies a calm, lake-like expanse, still and sheltered, except for the violent gusts which from time to time rush over the surface, at one time taking the vessel aback, and on the next occasion striking her on one quarter or the other unexpectedly. It is not a spot where the master of a sailing vessel could afford to go to sleep. At the western edge of this bay an anchorage has been obtained on a patch close to the shore. The walls of the crater are now clothed with vegetation up to the very summit. For the two thousand feet or so that they extend upwards the gardens of the natives peep out, recognized by their patches of yams in the presence of cocoanuts, palms, and bananas. There was a time within the memory of the Mission when the inhabitants were as wild and as quarrelsome as any in the entire district, and the Ureparapara bow, with its peculiar bend, has always been renowned. There are some heathens still, because it is so difficult to reach villages scattered everywhere both inside and outside this great horse-shoe, and apparently hanging on to the slopes by their eyelids. The lofty barrier of the crater walls is always a hindrance to rapid locomotion. In 1878, three scholars who had been to Norfolk Island returned; and a Mota man (named Viletuwale) started the first school. We have at the present time two schools, both excellently managed—one inside the crater, the other on the northern and outside face of the mountain.

The baptized number one hundred and twenty-three; the young scholars are sixty-seven; the total, including all listeners, is one hundred and seventy-eight, but one hundred and ninety heathen still remain scattered in inaccessible nooks. What also makes the work difficult is the fact that the villages here are so small. They form a chain of small communities on the slopes, sadly interfering with teaching; for there is no definite centre of population. A village consists in Ureparapara of a single house and one gamal. The house will be divided inside by low partitions, and in one of these a whole family sleeps. The young men are, of course, in the gamal. The mission is trying to improve this state of things, and to induce the natives (and with success) to give themselves more air and light. So much of the work of the Mission is done by native teachers, who are not naturally communicative, that it is not easy to give those indications of personal spiritual progress which are more easily obtained in places where the white man is always present. This is the answer to a criticism, which is naturally made, that the Melanesian Mission does not sufficiently give definite instances of the growth of spiritual life. But it will certainly interest my readers to peruse two letters which I give here. Let it be understood that none of the clergy knew anything of the matter till it was all over, but the letters fell into their hands afterwards. The two young men who wrote the letters were at the time scholars at Norfolk Island. One is now the teacher at the crater school in Ureparapara, the other has a like post in Florida in the Solomon Group. The letters will explain themselves. It was a quarrel, happily composed by the persons themselves without intervention. It arose through a misunderstanding. Of course the letters were written in "Mota."

"Norfolk Island, June 7, 1889.

"SIMON QALGES,

"My brother, is this word which I have heard true or not? They said that you said that you all would fight with me on fishing day (Saturday).

But is it consistent with the law of fellowship to fight or not? We all here have had fellowship together in Christ's religion. We have all received one baptism, and some of us have joined together in receiving the Holy Communion of the Body of Christ. And how shall we again have divisions amongst us who have been dwelling together in true brotherhood, according to the law of God? Now, to-day, did it appear to you that I was angry? No, I was not angry. But I was surprised to see you throwing at that little boy as if he were a grown person; and the boys belonging to us (Solomon Islanders) entreated me to let them go and help him; but I would not let them go, and they were angry with me for it; and then I saw you look as though you were angry, and I was going forward to speak to you, but it was all over. Now you and I are to partake of the Holy Communion on Sunday, if able; and, if there be fighting on Saturday, will that be good or not? The sun is nigh upon setting. Don't prolong this affair, my brother, because we are both brethren, and it is not right for us to act in such a manner.

"I, Herbert Kulai, have written in love."

Answer from Simon Qalges to the above:—

"Herbet Kulai to you all.

"The peace of our God be with us. This is my answer to your letter about what I did to-day to Kasi, because they said he was clever in dodging; so I pelted him to see if it were so. I thought it was all being done in play. Then I saw you coming towards me with a hoe in your hand, not as though peaceably, and it appeared to me that your minds were disturbed; but my mind was not at all disturbed. I thought it was only play; but you thought it was something different. But in what way have I caused dissension? And this I ask you: Who told you that word came out of my mouth? When we came back to-day did you think it was so? I did not. About that word that we should fight it out on Saturday they told me that it was talked over there; but I knew nothing at all about it. This I heard—that Tari-vaga and Garo told us that you people took a spear and called my name over it. But just all of you put that spear back in its place and then take up the Cross of Christ and hold it fast; and then let us fight manfully at the side of Christ all our days till death. My brother, tell them that if their minds are upset, it is for us two to pray that God will forgive. Tell this to those over there, and I will tell the boys over here. That is all.

"I, Simon Qalges, have written with very great love."

Such letters take us into the innermost spirit of the Mission work, for here the Christian teaching, which has been received by the scholars by the influence of the Holy Ghost, is evolved in the most natural of ways, by letters written in privacy. I do not think, now that years have passed, that I have violated the rules of delicacy in reproducing these documents as evidences that God's grace blesses the Mission, and permits them to see the fruit of their labours. It is affecting to note how the sons of those who knew no better return but that of vengeance for an insult once received, are now unwilling to let the sun go down upon their wrath. That meeting at the Holy Communion, after the quarrel had been made up, must have been the seal of a deeper and fuller corporate Christian life.

One subject I have not yet touched upon—that of cannibalism. It is believed that throughout the Banks Group this horrible practice has been unknown for a very long time, even if it ever existed. No one living seems to have been acquainted with it. This is all the more strange, because in the New Hebrides close by, there is no doubt that it exists still in some islands, and was the universal custom not many years ago. It has been unknown in the Santa Cruz group; probably it was never practised there; whereas in the Solomons there are at this moment tens of thousands of cannibals.

CHAPTER VIII.

THE RELIGION OF THE MELANESIANS.

THE following is taken from Dr. Codrington's work, "The Melanesians; their Anthropology and Folk-lore." 16s. (Clarendon Press.) It is a book which will be often quoted. The statement about Melanesian beliefs is so admirably put (if I may be permitted to say it) that I have copied it verbatim. Those who wish to obtain an intelligent knowledge of the natives in these regions would wish to realize, first and foremost, what are the ideas we wish to modify or displace in order to give them the Gospel of Christ.

"The religion of the Melanesians is the expression of their conception of the supernatural, and embraces a very wide range of beliefs and practices, the limits of which it would be very difficult to define. It is equally difficult to ascertain with precision what these beliefs are. The ideas of the natives are not clear upon many points, they are not accustomed to present them in any systematic form among themselves. An observer, who should set himself the task of making systematic inquiries, must find himself baffled at the outset by the multiplicity of the languages with which he has to deal. Suppose him to have as a medium of communication a language which he and those from whom he seeks information can use freely for the ordinary purposes of life, he finds that to fail when he seeks to know what is the real meaning of those expressions which his informant must needs use in his own tongue, because he knows no equivalent for them in the common language which is employed, or, if he gives what he supposes to be an equivalent, it will often happen that he and the inquirer do not understand that word in the same sense. A missionary has his own difficulty in the fact that very much of his communication is with the young, who do not themselves know and understand very much of what their elders believe and practise. Converts are disposed to blacken generally and indiscriminately their own former state, and with greater zeal the present practices of others. There are some things they are really ashamed to speak of, and there are others which they think they ought to consider wrong, because they are associated in their memory with what they know to be really bad. Many a native Christian will roundly condemn native songs and dances, who, when questions begin to clear his mind, acknowledges that some dances are quite innocent, explains that none that he knows have any religious significance whatever, says that many songs also have nothing whatever bad in them, and writes out one or two as examples. Natives who are still heathen will speak with reserve of what still retains with them a sacred character, and a considerate missionary will respect such reserve. If he should not respect it, the native may very likely fail in his respect for him, and amuse himself at his expense. Few missionaries have time to make systematic inquiries; if they do they are likely to make them too soon, and for the whole of their after career make whatever they observe fit into their early scheme of the native religion. Often missionaries, it is to be feared, so manage it that neither they nor the first generation of their converts really know what the old religion of the native people was. There is always with missionaries the difficulty of language; a man may speak a native language for years and have reason to believe he speaks it well, but it will argue ill for his real acquaintance with it if he does not find out that he makes mistakes. Resident traders, if observant, are free from some of a missionary's difficulties; but they have their own. The 'pigeon English,' which is sure to come in, carries its own deceits: 'plenty devil' serves to convey much information: a chief's grave is 'devil's stones,' the dancing ground of a village is a 'devil ground,' the drums are idols, a dancing club is a 'devil stick.'" Dr. Codrington adds in a note: "It may be asserted with confidence that a belief in a devil, that is of an evil spirit, has no place whatever in the native Melanesian mind. The word has certainly not been introduced in the Solomon or Banks Islands by missionaries, who in those groups have never used the word 'devil.' Yet, most unfortunately, it has come to pass that the religious beliefs of European traders have been conveyed to the natives in the word 'devil,' which they use without knowing what it means. It is much to be wished that educated Europeans would not use the word so loosely as they do." The most intelligent travellers and naval officers pass their short period of observation in this atmosphere of confusion. Besides, every one, missionary and visitor, carries with him some preconceived ideas.

He expects to see idols, and he sees them. Images are labelled idols in museums, whose makers carve them for amusement. A Solomon Islander fashions the head of his lime-box stick into a grotesque figure, and it becomes the subject of a woodcut as "a Solomon Island god."

"It is extremely difficult for any one to begin inquiries without some prepossessions, which, even if he can communimate with the natives in their own language, affect his conception of the meaning of the answers he receives. The questions he puts guide the native to the answer he thinks he ought to give. The native, with very vague beliefs and notions floating in cloudy solution in his mind, finds in the questions of the European a thread on which these will precipitate themselves, and without any intention to deceive, avails himself of the opportunity to clear his own mind while he satisfies the questioner. . . . The Melanesian mind is entirely possessed by the belief in a supernatural power or influence, called, almost universally, 'Mana.' This is what works to effect everything which is beyond the ordinary power of men outside the common processes of nature; it is present in the atmosphere of life, attaches itself to persons and to things, and is manifested by results which can only be ascribed to its operation. When one has got it he can use it and direct it, but its force may break forth at some new point; the presence of it is ascertained by proof. A man comes by chance upon a stone which takes his fancy; its shape is singular, it is like something, it is certainly not a common stone, there must be 'Mana' in it. So he argues with himself, and he puts it to the proof; he lays it at the root of a tree to the fruit of which it has a certain resemblance, or he buries it in the ground when he plants his garden; an abundant crop on the tree or in the garden shows that he is right, the stone is 'Mana,' has that power in it. Having that power it is a vehicle to convey 'Mana' to other stones. . . . In the same way certain forms of words, generally in the form of a song, have power for certain purposes; a charm of words is called a 'Mana.' But this power, though itself impersonal, is always connected with some person who directs it. . . . If a stone is found to have a supernatural power, it is because a spirit has associated itself with it; a dead man's bone has with it 'Mana' . . . a man may have so close a connection with a spirit or ghost, that he has 'Mana' in himself also. . . . Thus all conspicuous success is a proof that a man has 'Mana,' as he becomes a chief by virtue of it. Hence a man's power is his 'Mana.' The Melanesians believe in the existence of beings personal, intelligent, full of 'Mana,' with a certain bodily form which is visible, but not fleshly like the bodies of men. . . . These may be called spirits; but it is most important to distinguish between spirits who are beings of an order higher than mankind, and the disembodied spirits of men. . . . From the neglect of this distinction, great confusion arises. Any personal object of worship among natives in all parts of the world is taken by the European observer to be a spirit, or a god, or a devil; but among many Melanesians, at any rate, it is very common to invoke departed relatives and friends, and to use religious rites addressed to them. A man, therefore, who is approaching with some rite his dead father, whose spirit he believes to be existing and pleased with his pious action, is thought to be worshipping a false god or a deceiving spirit, and very probably is told that the being he worships does not exist. The perplexed native hears with one ear that there is no such thing as that departed spirit of a man which he venerates as a ghost that his instructor takes to be a god, and with the other that the soul never dies, and that his own spiritual interests are paramount and eternal.

"They themselves make a clear distinction between the existing, conscious, powerful, disembodied spirits of the dead, and other spiritual beings that never have been spirits at all. . . . There does not appear to be anywhere in Melanesia a belief in a spirit which animates any natural object, a tree, waterfall, storm, or rock, so as to be to it what the soul is believed to be to the body of a man; . . . the native idea is that ghosts haunt the sea and the forest, having power to raise storms. . . . It may be said that Melanesian religion divides the people into two groups, one, where, with an accompanying belief in spirits never seen, worship is directed to the ghosts of the dead, as in the Solomon Islands; the other, where both ghosts and spirits have an important place, but the spirits have more worship than the ghosts, as in the case of the New Hebrides and in the Banks Islands."

It would appear to me from all I have read that the Melanesian mind has never risen to the conception of one Supreme Being—the notion does not seem to have seized upon their imagination. Dr. Codrington adds the following important note: "The Melanesian Mission, under the guidance of Bishop Patteson, has used in all islands the English word *God*. He considered the enormous difficulty, if not impossibility, of finding an adequate native impression in any one language, and, further, the very narrow limits within which such a word, if it could be found, must be used, since the languages are at least as many as the islands. It is difficult to convey by description the ideas which ought to attach to the new word, but at least nothing erroneous is connoted by it."

How wise was the action thus taken, the members of the Mission have constantly realized. There is no doubt that missionaries in China and in New Zealand are regretting bitterly that a contrary decision was arrived at there. All words such as "sheep," "lamb," which naturally have no counterpart in Melanesia, have been preserved in their English form.

I will add here that no one can fail to be impressed by the wise and liberal sentiments of the author of "The Melanesians." It will give increased confidence to the supporters of the Mission, as well as attract other thoughtful men to give their assistance, when they realize the humility, and yet the keen insight of one who has done so much for the Mission as "Dr. Codrington."

In the Banks Islands a system of self-help has now been begun. If some missions have been criticized for exacting too much from new converts, we must blame the Melanesian Mission—if it is right to blame at all—for being too tender and careful. It has been almost entirely giving without receiving. But in aid of the self-denial movement for Missions in Australasia in 1894, Melanesians gave food and "curios" which realized more than one hundred and fifty pounds. In 1895 in the Banks Islands a system of monthly collections has been commenced, which promises well. In Santa Maria on one Sunday morning goods to the value of one pound twelve shillings were given. At Motalava on another Sunday one thousand seven hundred and ninety-five cocoanuts were presented, and were worth almost as much. These are specimens of the new spirit of self-help.

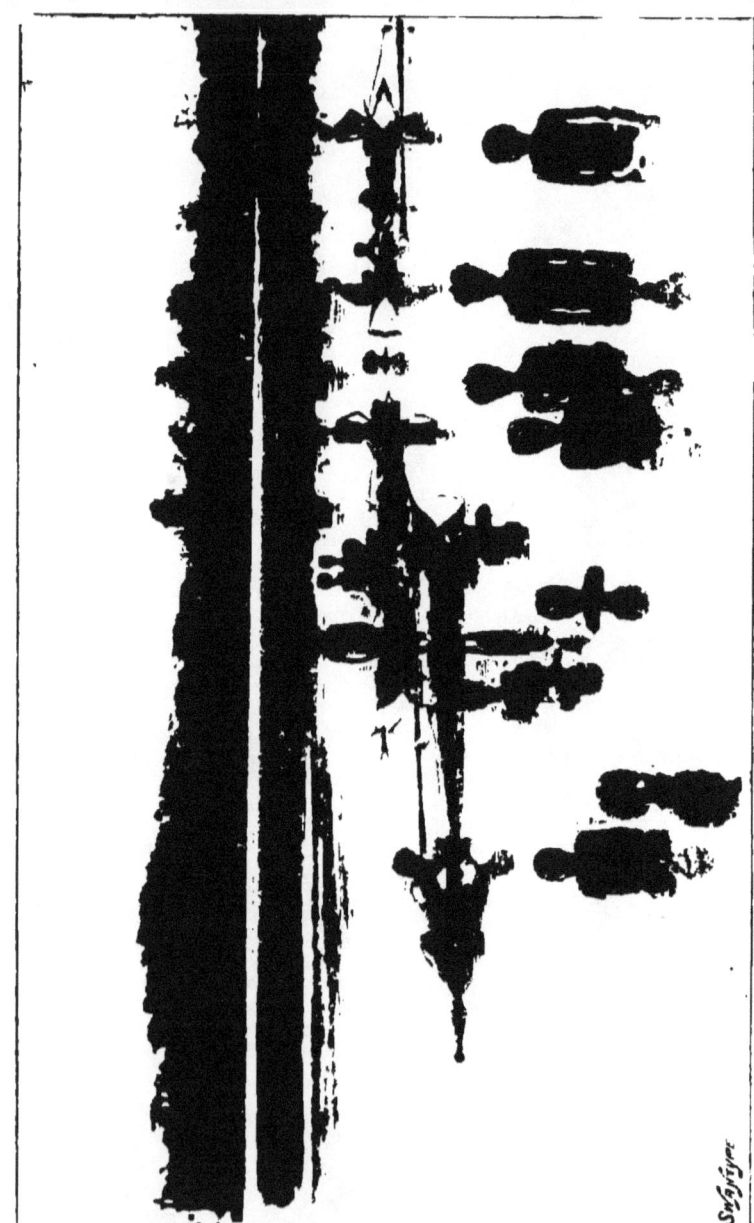

Children at Ka (Banks Island).

CHAPTER IX.

THE ISLAND OF MOTALAVA, TOGETHER WITH THE ADJOINING ISLAND OF RA.

NINE schools; one thousand and thirteen baptized; three hundred and thirteen scholars; one thousand and thirty-three listeners; no heathen; two native clergy. These two islands are under the charge of the Rev. Henry Tagalana and the Rev. Walter Woser.

North-east of Vanua Lava, and some six miles away, and eight miles from Mota, there is situated the island of Motlav or Motalava. Not so extensive as Vanua Lava, it has been completely won in Christ's name now for many years. Adjoining it, and connected with it by a reef of some quarter of a mile, is the little coral island of Ra. People can at any time, I think, walk across from one place to the other, though of course it means wading at times. Inside the highest point of reef, a shallow lagoon of about a mile in extent separates the two islands. It is a good fishing place, and at times the natives attempt to poison the whole area of it and thus catch great quantities of their favourite food. Bishop Selwyn, the elder, I believe, obtained boys from these places early during his visits. But it may be a long time before one of these lads becomes fitted to be a teacher, so that permanent work may be commenced. It often happens that boys will only remain in Norfolk Island for a year. This makes them practically useless, and they quickly drift back into their old ways, especially if there is no school in the place. I believe it is not more than twenty years since a school was first started at Motlav, in about 1871. Now there is quite a large band of communicants, some two hundred and fifty of them. There are nine schools, one thousand and thirteen baptized Christians, three hundred and thirteen young scholars in the schools, including those who are preparing for baptism, which means the entire population. The number under the influence of the Mission is one thousand and thirteen.

Since many are baptized as adults, my readers may well ask why not more than two hundred and ten have been confirmed, and are communicants? I have asked the question myself, and I think there is a feeling in the Mission that great efforts must be made to impart more fully that deeper teaching, which should follow after baptism, so that the members of the Church may be sustained by their full share in the Divinely appointed sacraments.

I am not criticizing the past action of the Mission. I have seen too much of the great extent of the field to be ignorant of the difficulties they have to contend with; often the teachers are not sufficiently qualified to give the fuller instruction, and when the number of schools is taken into consideration, as well as the difficulties of locomotion, it is no wonder that much he would desire to do is still left undone by the clergyman in charge. As the schools multiply and the baptized Christians increase in number, it is certain that there must be at least two white clergymen in each group. At present one white clergyman has for his jurisdiction the whole Banks Group, numbering some ten islands, with their forty-two or forty-three schools.

But to return to Motlav and Ra. The principal figure in the community here is the Rev. Henry Tagalana. He is the oldest of a family of nine— eight of whom have been taught at Norfolk Island. Four still live, and are all engaged in teaching. Henry came to Kohimarama, in Auckland, in 1862, then moved to Norfolk Island in 1866, and remained there three years. After this he returned to open a school at Ra. He was ordained deacon in 1873, and priest a few years afterwards. He is a man of strong character, and much respected. He makes his influence felt throughout his area of work, and he often goes to Vanua Lava to inspect and strengthen the schools there. Just across the reef which leads to Motlav we reach a village where the Rev. Walter Woser lives. Walter came as a very little boy to Kohimarama about 1865. In due time he returned, and started a school at Motlav, his home. In 1886 he was ordained deacon. It will be seen then that Motlav and Ra are favoured by the presence of two native clergymen, one a priest, and the other a deacon. In Motlav, as in so many islands, different parts are inhabited by natives who have special dialects. At the west end of the island, at Valuwa, the people are different from those living at Ra, and where Walter Woser is. They are being taught by teachers from the neighbourhood of the two native clergy. As a practical example of the working of the Holy Spirit among these people, inducing them to think of their neighbours, and to take trouble in the hour of distress, I ought to relate how, quite early in the history of the Mission, about the year 1872, the news came to Motlav that the Mota people were suffering from a scarcity of food. Now, very little food grows in Motlav itself; it does not abound either in good land or in much water. But the Christians were determined to aid their brethren, just as we hear in the Acts of the Apostles the Churches of Asia made a collection for the Christians at Jerusalem and sent it by the hands of St. Paul as a practical sign of good-will. They made a collection on a certain Sunday, and having no food of their own to spare, they sailed across to Vanua Lava, bought food there, and took it over for the relief of their brethren at Mota, where the Rev. George Sarawia was struggling with many difficulties after the martyrdom of his bishop, and after death from disease and a hurricane preceding the epidemic had worked sad havoc among his people.

There are no very striking characteristics in the physical features of Motlav. It is, I think, larger than Mota; it has a volcanic range in the centre also, with flat land bordering on the sea. I cannot, however, omit to chronicle a story told me by a trader at Motlav. Some one was giving a lecture on the beauties of the South Sea Islands, and in the course of his description of them he said that the remarkable fact about these islands was that they were wholly surrounded by the sea! Any one who has seen one coral island has seen them all, so far as their colouring from a distant view is concerned. Everywhere there is a dense mass of the greenest vegetation. The general appearance does not vary in summer or winter. Big clumps rising against the sky-line are sure to be banian trees. The lighter greens are pretty certain to be cocoanut palms. Here and there trees of a very light green, or even yellow, are noticed. These are a kind which afford leaves which taste like lettuce, and often indicate from some distance the presence of a village. It is not often that in the Banks Islands any villages are visible from the sea. As a rule they are a few hundred yards inland, for the sake of concealment, I suppose, and also so as to be sheltered from hurricanes. In the Banks Islands a creeping vine, very tenacious of life, overgrows all the trees, and destroys the individuality of the landscape. These creepers hang like a wall over the forest-clad slopes of hills, and give a flat look to the vegetation. In these more southern islands there are no open spaces of pasture land. Here and there, and often in the steepest spots, brown openings reveal the yam gardens of the natives. Except for fantastic shapes of extinct volcanoes, the visitor feels that when he has viewed one of these islands he has seen them all—the same green forests and the same thin line of coral sand along the shore, with overhanging trees. Nor in this locality is the coral the beautiful object that books speak of. I never saw under water anything except what looked like brown masses of rock with a feathered edge, and often the rock masses are like huge brown sea anemones. In Fiji and elsewhere, the branching coral is more frequent.

If you stand on Motlav and look towards Vanua Lava, you notice a hill, not far from the sulphur springs which send their steam into the air; this is called the hill of Qat. Qat is the theme of the fairy tales of the natives. Dr. Codrington says he is not a god, though he is more than a man. "He is certainly not the lord of the spirits. He is the hero of story-tellers; the ideal character of a good-natured people who profoundly believe in magic, and greatly admire adroitness and success in the use of it. Qat himself is good-natured, only playfully mischievous, and thoroughly enjoys the exercise of his wonderful powers. . . . It is difficult for the story-tellers to keep him distinct from ordinary men, though they always insist that he was a vui (spirit); and though he certainly never was a man, the people of the place where he was born, in Vanua Lava, Alosepere, claim him as their ancestor." Dr. Codrington gives many stories about him as they were narrated by the Rev. Edwin Wogale, a native deacon now dead, who was of the Sepere stock. I cannot disentangle these to give an intelligible specimen of them in a manner to interest those who have not a minute acquaintance with the islands, and their products, and their customs. But it would appear that Qat has now left the world. It was from Santa Maria that he took his departure. "Where now in the centre of that island is the great lake, there was formerly a plain covered with forest. Qat cut himself a large canoe there out of one of the largest trees. While making it he was often ridiculed by his brothers, and asked how he would ever get so large a canoe to the sea. He answered always that they would see by-and-by. When the canoe was finished he took inside it his wife and brothers, collected the living creatures of the island, even those so small as ants, and shut himself with them inside the canoe, to which he had made a covering. Then came a deluge of rain, the great hollow of the island became full of water, which burst through the surrounding hills where now descends the great waterfall of Gaua. The canoe tore a channel for itself out to sea, and disappeared. The people believed that the best of everything was taken from the islands when Qat so left them, and they looked forward to his return. When for the first time Bishop Patteson and his companions went ashore at Mota, some of the natives now living remember that it was said that Qat and his brothers were returned. Some years after that, a small trading vessel ran on the reef at Gaua and was lost. The old people, seeing her apparently standing into the channel of the waterfall stream, cried out that Qat was come again, and that his canoe knew her way home. It is likely now that the story will be told of eight persons in the canoe; but it is certain that the story is older than any knowledge of Noah's ark among the people.

THE ISLAND OF ROWA (BANKS GROUP).

One school; thirty-eight baptized; eighteen scholars; thirty-eight inhabitants.

It would be impossible to present a greater contrast than that which subsists between two adjacent islands in this group—between Ureparapara and Rowa. Only a few miles separate them. The former is nothing but a huge volcano without level surfaces, except of the narrowest along the water's edge. Rowa is a flat coral island; all round it extends a huge barrier reef, extending for miles into the sea. Sailing through the channels in the coral is exciting work where it is possible, because at any moment one may strand upon a rough edge, which does not improve the boat's planking. Round the actual island is a stretch of shallow water, which literally swarms with fish. Upon the occasion when I visited these shores, I saw along the beach a number of men up to their knees in water, stalking silently about with bows and arrows, every now and then taking a sudden aim and shooting into the water. By this means they catch quantities of fish; and there are no better fish for the table, a sort of silver mullet white as salmon trout. The people here are all Christians, and are all baptized. They number thirty-eight; and of these eighteen are in the school as young learners. Their life from the Mission point of view has been an uneventful one. Those who have slept upon the island say that the mosquitoes are famed for their ferocity. Indeed, among the sand—for there is little else but sand—such creatures swarm in myriads; a clump of cocoanuts and tropical bush hides the school-house, but there are no gardens here. The people of Rowa catch their fish and take them over to Vanua Lava and exchange them there for yams and other vegetables. Close to Rowa we saw an island in process of formation. Upon the shallow reef we observed one solitary cocoanut tree, looking as if it were actually growing in the water. It is the nucleus of what will certainly become another Rowa. By that time Rowa will have enlarged her borders and will probably possess a larger population. The teacher here is a remarkable character and a great boatman. There is, I believe, one solitary point of rock on this flat sandy island. It tells of the centre round which the sand collected and the coral grew. Whether it is the top of an old volcano gradually sinking down I cannot say.

CHAPTER X.

THE TORRES GROUP OF ISLANDS.

FIVE islands, one uninhabited; five schools; one hundred and twenty-four baptized; eighty-nine scholars; four hundred and eighty attending church; total population not accurately known.

Some fifty miles north of Ureparapara, which is the northern outpost of the Banks Islands, we come to a little group of islands, one of which is uninhabited. "They lie pretty well in a straight line, almost north and south. The southernmost is Toga, next to which is Lo. Then we come to Tëgua; next to this lies Metame, which is uninhabited, but used by the Teguans for gardens. Lastly, and northernmost, is Hiw."

In 1880, Bishop Selwyn visited nearly all of these, and the Rev. E. Wogale, a native deacon, was placed in charge. Before this, Wogale had been in Fiji instructing the Melanesians who had been taken there in labour vessels. All accounts of these islands speak of the scarcity of water. There appear to be no running streams, and the people are dependent for their supplies upon holes in the rock and upon a few springs, which, being below high-water mark, are brackish. Whether it is the absence of fresh water or from some other cause, it is certain that the natives here are more given than any others—though all are subject to them—to a species of sore, generally on the legs. They assume enormous proportions, and are terrible looking objects. The native name for them is "maniga;" and I have been informed by Dr. Welchman that they differ from such sores as Europeans are accustomed to have. When the bishop landed in 1880, the cry was, "Look out the manigas!" And the first duty was to become a doctor. Unfortunately the natives are most careless about dressing their wounds. They will go into salt water with them thoughtlessly, and no action could be more foolish. They will not take the trouble to fetch water daily to wash the wound. The disease very often seizes children, but they have greater recuperative power, and are more easily cured. If an adult is afflicted with the complaint, and is not careful, death has been known to ensue in a few days, I suppose from mortification. The Torres Islanders have always been reckoned as some of the fiercest and most savage. Bishop Selwyn's account of the moral condition of the natives in 1880 is that of the twenty-five villages in Tëgua all were jealous of each other as well as of any one who ventured to call at any other village besides their own. These villages consisted, on an average, of about twenty-four persons. But the bishop went to his task in the spirit of Christian hope. He adds, "Popular opinion says that savage nature will hold its own till it is swept away. Christ speaks to us of a death unto sin, and a new birth unto righteousness."

In 1883 the Rev. E. Wogale died at Vava, on

the island of Lo, where the first school had been opened. In the next year Robert Pantutun began work here. He is a Mota man, though his wife is a native of Lo. The bishop also took some boys with him, in 1880, to Norfolk Island. Two of these were brothers, and are now teachers, William Wulenew and Ernest Tughur. Robert Pantutun is a deacon. He was one of Bishop Patteson's earliest scholars, and has been a steady worker for years. His son John is in this year (1892) the organist of the chapel at Norfolk Island, and most striking it is to watch a Melanesian in that beautiful little church, a boy with frizzly head and bare feet, making full use of the pedals, and playing with taste and feeling the music of most of the great composers of sacred music. It can easily be realized what a deprivation it is to these native organists when they return to their homes as teachers, and are debarred from the use of musical instruments, for no harmonium has yet been invented which will stand the damp and the insect pests of these tropical islands.

The Torres Islands show long ere their shores are reached their coralline formation. When they are only blue masses on the horizon their outlines reveal successive flat terraces rising as a series of steps till at the highest point they are merged into a rocky bluff, round which, I suppose, the coral was originally formed. Successive upheavals in distant ages will, I imagine, account for these raised beaches, which are now covered with vegetation, and have been for ages untouched by the ocean swell. Those who know this group best tell us that a great many of the adult population have been taken by labour vessels, leaving, only too often, the old and the very young on the islands, and checking the due cultivation of the gardens.

A story is told how a class which was being prepared for baptism by the Rev. Robert Pantutun went down on one occasion to the shore to look at a labour vessel, but with no intention of going away in her; but suddenly one of their number jumped into the recruiters' boat, and he was followed by the whole class. Who can help sympathizing with the feelings of the teacher, whether white or black? What would any clergyman of a settled English parish say were the whole of his confirmation candidates to be suddenly lured away from him to be taken to a land where perhaps there was no church and no clergyman, where possibly no one knew their language, and where they would associate with some white men who did not even care to call themselves Christians, and whose lives would not bear inspection? The change to such a locality which might be their lot would be a great contrast to their old life, where the only white man they knew was a missionary. Of course, the dark picture I have drawn of a plantation is only a possible reflection of the truth. That it is not universally true the members of the Melanesian Mission will be the first to acknowledge. They know of schools for the islanders in the Brisbane diocese. They have among their best teachers returned labourers, as at Merig. They see these men take their places in large numbers in the schools on their return, having seen much evil, but having, by the providence of God, been kept from it. Whilst, then, we can all sympathize with the teachers when they lose their most advanced scholars—is there not also another aspect of the case? Can life be all-satisfying in an island which is almost waterless, where sores of a most virulent type are so common that an individual can hardly hope to escape them? Or, again, if the Christian teacher opens the eyes of natives to wonders of which he has not heard before, speaks of strange animals, mighty navies, machinery, cathedrals for the worship of God, exhibits pictures of these, and thus opens their understandings, is it not likely that some of those who have most deeply imbibed his instruction will be just those who may be most quickly drawn to wish to see the world for themselves? Theirs is a case analogous to the young man whom fond parents desire to keep at home, safe, as they think, from the temptations of an evil world, and they are grieved beyond measure because one day he runs away or speaks his mind and wishes to depart. It is a not unnatural course, and as wise parents make up their minds to the inevitable, and set to work to prepare their sons to meet evil and to conquer it, so I believe it should be in the islands of the South Seas. It is wiser to be prepared to see the natives departing to see the world, to prepare them for that world, and to use all our influence to get the regulations of the labour traffic conscientiously carried out. An attitude of passive antagonism is not calculated to succeed in the end. The views I here enunciate have been arrived at by me after much consultation. They are also the views, I think, of some of the members of the Melanesian Mission. They are not blind opponents of the system of recruiting for Queensland and Fiji. I may say, also, that I began my voyage in the *Southern Cross* somewhat prejudiced against the labour traffic, and, therefore, my present opinions may fairly be claimed as the result of actual experience in the centres from which the labour for Queensland is obtained. And I refuse to believe that the people of Queensland will in future forget their responsibilities to these children of the world—for such they are—whom they have with open eyes invited to live in their midst. To be careless of their best welfare would be a crime analogous to that of a man who deliberately invites to his house a young and an inexperienced boy, and who then, either thoughtlessly or wilfully, corrupts that lad's nature or ill-treats him. There is no one possessed of even the smallest share of our common humanity whose blood does not boil at the prospect of such a sin. May God keep the English nation, or any portion of it, from ever being convicted of it in the future. That we have been guilty of it, perhaps from carelessness or inattention, there can be no doubt whatever. But I believe that period is past, so far as our English possessions are concerned, and we are looking for the dawn of a brighter day. Planters are often impatient with the dulness of their black labourers, or are angry because they do not work with the vigour and capacity of English navvies. It would be wiser if they remembered, first, that the medium of communication is not the native languages, but that vilest of compounds that ever polluted the purity of speech, named "pigeon English," a dialect which may well take some time to master. But, secondly, and chiefly, Englishmen would do well to remember that their wonderful supremacy throughout the world is due in great measure to the existence of races inferior to their own. Were these black races as superior as they would like them to be in the sugar fields, it is certain that we should not be holding an immense tract of Africa, nor even the South Seas, nor North America, nor, though it is a very different race, should we be in India at all. Such reflections may well teach us to be patient with qualities which in some degree are characteristic of those whose lands we have seized, and whose services we have laid under contribution at the expense to ourselves of very low wages. My belief in a properly regulated labour traffic in the future, one which may tend to the advantage of both the black and the white, rests upon the fact that now at last the fearful evils of the past have been laid bare. It is *after* this stage, and not before, that English rule among dark coloured races becomes beneficent. It is *after* the public voice of the press and of the pulpit, and the exertions of Christian people are directed to one common end, that I believe in the justice and humanity of British rule. Before this stage has been reached the English race is capable of great brutality. I mean that single specimens of our race left to themselves, outside the reach of public opinion and not responsible to any Government, have been guilty of a brutality which can only be explained by a belief in a callousness to pain and to good feelings, which, to some among us, may seem incredible. Speaking as an Englishman, I believe my own race is capable of a vulgarity, a coarseness, and an obtuseness to a sense of beauty, which astonish nimbler and quicker peoples. Who that has watched the British tourist on classic soil in foreign lands can doubt what I say? And this coarseness becomes savagery in many an isolated trader or settler far from religious influences and family ties. It has led to the awful history of wrong in the past to the Australian aboriginal, to the South Sea Islander, and the North American Indian. But I also believe that the British nature, so dense and coarse as it can be, is also capable of the highest polish, close-grained as it is, and with the best of possibilities in its heart of hearts. I would trust an English statesman before any other. I believe in the justice of a right-minded English settler before the representative of any other nation. When once we are roused to the sense of our shortcomings, I believe we Englishmen will make fuller reparation and embody it in a purer legislation than any other nationality. For these reasons, whilst I have not hesitated to bring a heavy indictment against my own people, I believe that we can, and we certainly shall, consult in the future the best interests of the South Sea Islanders, and that the labour traffic can be a great means of civilization and a help to the Mission, in spite of that awful past which makes us positively shudder. Whether any who have had personal experience of the brutal days in the South Seas can ever be brought to believe in the dawn of a better era is another question. I doubt if they can.

"In the Torres Islands they have a method of honouring the dead, which is striking. They rear close to their houses little erections like altars, on which may be seen a few skulls. These are the remains of relatives. A few yams or a cocoanut are placed alongside them, but not as a sacrifice. They are memorials of affection, used as we are in the habit of using flowers on graves. They keep green the memory of any person of importance for a great length of time, sometimes holding a great feast so long afterwards as the thousandth or even the two thousandth day of his death. When a man dies certain days are at once fixed and called 'Death Days,' such as the fifth, tenth, twentieth, fiftieth, and so on. The people meet and eat and drink kava till morning. As soon as possible after death the body is placed on a platform not far from the gamal, and is hidden from view by a screen of bamboos and sugar-cane. The people blacken their foreheads, and for ten days do not leave the village. From the fourth to the sixth day the atmosphere is usually unbearable, and they then place a sprig of a very strong-smelling herb through their nose-rings, which are pieces of bamboo placed in the cartilage, sometimes distending it to the diameter of an inch. On the tenth day the screen is taken down and burnt, and every one in the village takes the ashes and rubs them on his chest and forehead. This may not be washed off till a day then fixed, usually about the tenth day afterwards again. Then four of the men of the highest rank in the village take the head from the body, and, singing a doleful chant, march with it down to the sea, followed at a distance of about a quarter of a mile by all the people who have assembled for the occasion. They wash the head thoroughly, and return with the skull, which is then placed in the highest division in the gamal. It is the duty of the relatives to clear the path to the sea, and one finds in these islands what is apparently unknown in any other part of Melanesia, namely, a great broad road, cleared of all bush, and leading from the villages to the sea. After this ceremony the other remains are placed in a small walled enclosure, and are left there. When wanted, the leg and arm-bones are taken to make arrow tips. The natives of the Torres group are not cannibals, and have no tradition of any such custom."

It can easily be imagined how hard it often is to get words suitable for expressing spiritual teaching. This difficulty occurred in these islands about the word for prayer. They have a term which they use for "invoking" any ghost. This word had been incorporated into the Prayer-book for these people. At first they were puzzled, for they knew that we believe in one God only. After a long talk, lasting all night, in their gamal, they came in the morning to say that they had determined in future never to use that word except in reference to the true and one only God. This was a step gained, indeed.

On the island of Tëgua, a returned labourer, who had been instructed in the plantations in a Sunday-school, was most anxious to begin school among his own people. He was informed that he must first go to Lo and be instructed there in the baptismal class till the *Southern Cross* returned, when he could be baptized. It happened to be at the busiest time of the year, when every one was clearing the ground for the crops. This was pointed out to him. Still he persisted. "Take me and teach me; I must help here." "What about your gardens?" "My wife will look after those; she is a good worker." "And who will look after your wife?" He paused and said, "Yes, I do not like leaving her; but——" after another pause, and with a bright look, he said, "I think God will look after her: do you think He will?" "Yes," was the answer. And so this man made his venture of faith; and I doubt not that, having begun well, his labours will be abundantly blessed. There are now two schools in this group; one hundred and twenty-four persons have been baptized. There are eighty-nine young scholars in the school. The total number of listeners is four hundred and eighty. But I had no means of discovering what proportion this bears to the total population.

One hot and brilliant morning I landed at Vava, and made the acquaintance of the Rev. Robert Pantutun. But my first introduction to the place was the arrival of the captain in the saloon, loaded with bows, arrows, and clubs. "Here, bishop," he said, "you are to have the first chance this time." Most gladly did I pay their price in tobacco, for both the clubs and the arrows of the Torres Islanders are remarkable. The clubs are made of wood like ebony, and are rounded as though worked in a lathe; the arrows are pointed with long and very slender pieces of human bone. Vava is one of the places where the *Southern Cross* takes in wood, and a great pile was awaiting us on the reef. The road up to the village was broad and open, according to the custom of the people, for the sake of their burial rites. The church in this village is beautifully built, and is perhaps better appointed than any in these parts. Mr. Robin was away, and therefore there were no confirmations, but upon our return Robert Pantutun hoped to present a class of adults for baptism. In due time we anchored here again upon our return journey. The heat was great once more. Mr. Palmer baptized the catechumens, and I confess that I felt a malicious satisfaction in watching Palmer's uneasiness in using the Vava language. I may say here that one of my recurring anxieties was the language in which I had to confirm. At each spot I had to procure the prayer-book and get up an entirely new dialect. Getting into a corner, I proceeded to read over and over again the strange words and to catch the pronunciation by constant reference to the clergyman in charge. There was not always much time, but it was extremely important that the service should be in a language intelligible to the congregation. All I could do was to mark certain words and put in many commas so as to be sure in what part of the sentence I was; perhaps my greatest apprehension was lest I should miss a line and proceed regardless of the fact. Naturally I gave my whole mind to my task, and I believe I may say that not only did I make no serious blunder, but I was also fairly intelligible; this alone is great praise. I was able to read every dialect where there was a confirmation except in Santa Cruz. He would be a bold man who would attempt the Cruzian tongue without months of practice. When Palmer, then at Vava was in difficulties in the baptismal office—Palmer, too! the great Mota linguist—I could not refrain from a feeling of wicked satisfaction. Perhaps it was the indulgence of this evil habit which was the reason why I was visited by a plague equal to one of the plagues of Egypt. Suddenly, and during the course of the service, a cloud of blow flies appeared and made a dead set at me. Whether it was my shining poll—so unusual a sight in the Torres Islands—or whether they wished to inspect a bishop, I know not, but for the space of several minutes it was all I could do to keep from rushing out of the building; the flies formed a cordon round my head and face, and I could not drive them away, wild gesticulations and flappings of a prayer-book not being *comme il faut*.

CHAPTER XI.

SUQE—CHARMING.

INSERT here a deeply interesting account by the Rev. L. P. Robin of the custom called Suqe as it obtains in this group. Here it is called "Huqa."

"This is a kind of brotherhood to which all males above a certain age belong; women are rigidly excluded. As regards the Torres Islands, I am not aware of anything distinctly immoral in the rites of initiation or profession, but some are exceedingly nasty. During the rites, which last sometimes for eight or ten days, the people engaged confine themselves entirely to the village where the ceremony is going on, and to the sacred and secret spaces belonging to it. In cases of initiation the whole male population of the village takes part; but of course in those of progression to higher ranks, only those belonging to the higher ranks are present. After the separation of the sexes, the salient feature of the Suqe is the rigid laws regarding eating and drinking. In every village there are on one side of an open space the ordinary family huts; opposite to them on the other side is the gamal or Suqe hut. This is an immense hut some seventy or eighty feet in length. Inside it is divided into some eight or nine spaces, marked off by pieces of bamboo laid down at the divisions. In each space there are usually three native ovens or fireplaces. Down the centre lie long bamboos filled with water, each space has its own, supported near the open end by a forked stick. In or near each bamboo stand beautifully polished cocoanut cups, from which the natives drink. Gea, which resembles the Fijian kava, though not prepared in the same way, is drunk. Near each fireplace is the heap of stones used in cooking. Overhead, upon cross-beams, lie the various dishes, oven covers, etc., used in the preparation of the food. Stuck in the thatch are the finely carved wooden and tortoiseshell knives with which the mashed food is cut up and distributed. Near at hand lie the pestles or mashers, also with carved handles. Everywhere, hanging within easy reach, or propped against the sides of the hut, are to be seen bows and numbers of deadly bone-tipped arrows. Such is the interior of a gamal in the Torres Islands. The space nearest the entrance is open to children and the uninitiated; after that each space marks a higher rank, till the highest of all is reached at the extreme end of the hut. Now the Torres Suqe law is that no man may eat anywhere except in that space and at that oven which belongs to his rank. He may not eat fruit in his garden. He may on no account, unless very seriously ill, eat food in his own house with his wife or family, or that has been cooked or even touched by them. He may not touch the food, drink, or utensils of any one of higher or lower rank than himself. He may not even obtain fire, or its materials, from any but one of the same rank. If in passing up the gamal to his own place, he inadvertently touches the utensils belonging to any space through which he passes, he pays a fine. He may eat no food cooked in an oven other than that belonging to his rank. The same rules apply to drink. In his garden he alone digs his own yams for his meal and carries them home. The dishes, cups, etc., belonging to a man of very high rank may not be even *seen* by those of low rank. Outside the gamal it is proper to pay a certain deference to the head man. Thus a boy or man of low rank would never pass upright in front of a man of very high rank. They bow down. There is a kind of sanctity attaching to the head men—a sort of power supposed to be inherent in them by reason of their position, but which is not under their own control. In Torres this power, which is supposed to avenge any insult offered to the chief, is called the 'Her-hia.'

"Now, from the strictness of these rules, it was necessary to make the rejection or surrender of Suqe rank a condition of baptism. Because, since every baptized Christian must be potentially a communicant, this cutting off from eating in common was irreconcilable with the profession. And this was the chief difficulty with which we found we must deal at the outset. The man who broke the Suqe rules, and such was always extremely rare, was looked upon with contempt by the rest. He was considered a low fellow, no gentleman, and quite outside the pale. In fact, he lost caste, and could not recover his position. It was, therefore, a very critical test of a man's sincerity if he voluntarily threw up the *Suqe* to become a candidate for holy baptism. In the Banks Islands these rules are not nearly so strict, and no caste is lost by a man occasionally eating elsewhere than in his gamal place. But the secret ceremonies of initiation and the like are still carried on, and at times everything of a Church nature falls to the ground through the enforced seclusion of a whole village and their friends for some eight or ten days whilst these rites are being performed. With this trouble taking place in the Banks Islands, for a warning, I determined, if possible, to abolish the thing at Torres from the commencement. But it was of course no easy matter. However, in the first year seven men, headed by a man of the second rank, threw up the Suqe, and placed themselves under instruction for Holy Baptism. This good example was followed by others year by year, but no chief of the first degree could persuade himself to be the first to abrogate his position. And so there were four men in this rank, three of whom were very old, and from the first resolutely cut themselves off from all communication with us. The fourth, whilst friendly and professedly desirous to join us, insisted on two conditions being observed before he would himself take the decisive step; he stipulated (1) that all the natives of lower rank should break their Suqe *before* or at the same time as himself; (2) that the other chiefs of equal rank should do the same. His three fellow chiefs on the Island of Lo died. He and a residuum of some forty natives of second, third, and fourth ranks still held out.

"The sequel is most striking. The chiefs ate themselves out of the Suqe. Curiously enough they have made a rule about it, namely, that any one intending to do so, shall descend grade by grade, eating in each place and at each oven till he reaches the space near the door, where the little boys who have not been initiated eat. Then a great feast takes place outside with the women. During my visit, Tëqalqal, with a number of others who joined him as he reached their grades, did this. I always made a point when possible of attending both the last meal at the entrance space in the gemal, and also of course the great feast outside. On the occasion of Tëqalqal's last gamal meal (the gradual descent of course took several days), after all was over we got up, and every one together gave a great shout, making the welkin ring indeed. Then three cheers started by myself, and then a succession of the Torres whoop, which for penetrating powers, loudness, and hideousness, rivals any sound I know, including an Australian's coo-ee and a syren-whistle.

"Is there not something inexpressibly touching and also wonderful in this quite literal illustration of our blessed Lord's words, 'Except ye be converted and become as little children, ye shall not enter into the kingdom of heaven'? What but the Holy Spirit could have inspired these men to thus humble themselves to the very ground before their people, ay, and amid the sneers and scoffs of many who would not join? Truly it was an awe-inspiring thing to see, for one seemed to *feel* the breath of God about one, and to hear the still small voice speaking to the heart of this man and his friends. And besides the setting aside of his rank, there was more. By his high position the chief is supposed to be endued with some sort of special power and to be sacred, but over this power he himself has no control; but if it, in his person, is insulted, the people fear some punishment. Consequently they besought him, for his sake and theirs, not to do this thing lest they should all suffer for it. But in faith he did it, and many took courage and followed him; and on such a rock as *that* are the foundations of Christ's Church laid at Tëgua."

So interesting are Mr. Robin's observations, that I give the account of another custom in his words.

"Very different from the Suqe and death customs was another which it was necessary strenuously to oppose and, if possible, to eradicate from the outset. *Charming*, that is, at least, the *intention* to inflict death or disease upon an enemy, I found to be rife in Torres. The manner in which it is done is briefly this. A quarrels with B. A makes a charm. He takes a piece of a certain kind of wood, about two inches long. On each side of it he places a piece of a human rib. He binds the three tightly together; then he goes out, and conceals it very carefully in a path along which he knows his enemy is coming. B comes along and unsuspectingly passes over the hidden charm. A, who has concealed himself in the bush near at hand, comes out as soon as B has gone by, takes up the charm and goes home. He then waits for an opportunity of sending the charm away to a wizard. He is careful to send it to one on another island. An opportunity occurs, and A sends the charm to the wizard C, telling him to inflict death or disease upon B. C sets to work; fasts almost entirely from food for forty days, drinks nothing, and conducts his actual operations on the charm with the utmost secrecy. The process differs, of course, according to the punishment desired to be inflicted. But there are two main divisions, those meant to inflict death, and those meant to inflict disease. The disease charm is carried on uninterruptedly, and consists in winding the charm up in numerous layers of coarse cobwebs, leaves of particular plants, and here and there the long sharp thorns of the Tomago, which are fastened in with intention to inflict pains in particular parts of the victim's body, according to their position in the charm and the special incantations used in their insertion. The death charm, on the other hand, is worked on more slowly and at regular intervals; the object being apparently not to cause death too quickly, but to waste the victim away by two or three attacks upon his health first. This charm is also made with greater care. Only the very finest cobwebs are used; it is never allowed to get cold; in the intervals of working it is placed in a small piece of bamboo together with some powdered human bone, and hung over a fire which is never allowed to go out. Did the charm once get cold, the power in it would be lost. There are various stages in the working of the charm, which it would take much too long to enumerate and detail in this paper, and of which also I am myself not very well informed; the whole business being carried on with such secrecy that even where it is discontinued, it is excessively difficult to hear anything about it. As to whether there *is* a power exercised by these men, I give my own opinion for what it is worth; reminding you of what I said at the beginning of this paper, that many years are necessary to gain a definite knowledge of the intricate customs of the natives; also that it is extremely difficult to ascertain and certify given dates and coincidences. Yet I will say there is something quite incomprehensible to me in the charming, and quite irreconcilable with any theory of the death or illness being caused by fear. I see no cause to disbelieve, in fact, it seems to me reasonable, that Satan, in whose bond they are as heathen, should be able to bestow a hurtful power upon some of them. And I am emboldened to say this, since I heard Mr. Baring Gould say publicly in a lecture in England that the powers of the Zulu wizards are utterly inexplicable on any other theory than that of diabolical possession, or the co-operation of evil spirits. In any case the practice is, on the face of it, a wicked one; and it is at least suggestive and hopeful that it does not seem difficult to convince the natives that it is so. It is now entirely discontinued at Lo, and I think at Tëgua also. The other two islands are comparatively untouched as yet.

"In conclusion let me say that it is, I feel sure, most necessary to realize that these customs constitute the religion of the natives and of their forefathers. In endeavouring, therefore, to eradicate or supplant them, one should try to deal gently, gradually, and with tact, concerning them. The more delicately one handles such subjects, the more sympathetically one treats those whose manners and customs they are, the sooner will the natives learn to trust one, and the more easy will it be to persuade them in time to give up all those things which are either directly contrary to God's law, or obstacles in the way of a consistent following of it."

The "Southern Cross" off Santa Cruz.

CHAPTER XII.

THE SANTA CRUZ GROUP.

ONLY three schools at present; eighty-eight baptized; two hundred and fifty listeners.

Interesting as the Banks Islands are, there is no doubt, in my opinion, that the natives of Santa Cruz and of the Solomons have attracted me to a still higher degree. But this is owing in great measure to the fact that these northern regions are inhabited by natives still wild and untaught. The Banks Islanders are nearly all Christians; their native weapons are almost entirely thrown aside, and cannibalism was perhaps never practised. But as the *Southern Cross* sails northward she comes into waters far less known; the people are not only savage but wild, and to the mere traveller the romance of the situation is greater. I feel, in writing the pages that are to come, something of the excitement returning to me which I experienced when I first sighted the shores of Santa Cruz. I was conscious I was approaching a world but little visited, and where death had claimed many a victim from among the Mission band. I knew also that I was to behold a different race of men. The Torres Islands are the limit from the south of the kava-drinking native. Henceforth I was to witness the betel-chewing people. The natural mouth was to be exchanged for the lips reddened with juices, and teeth blackened with their favourite condiment. It was deeply interesting to know also that, except for the visit of an occasional war vessel, no ship approaches these shores except the *Southern Cross*. Here traders never come; here also the labour vessels never touched till quite lately; for though the men display a splendid physique, finer than that of any other race that I met, still they seem unable to bear transplanting. Even at Norfolk Island the Cruzian boys cause the greatest anxiety. They sicken quickly, and die suddenly. They are also by far the most excitable of any of these races; and warships exercise a wise discretion in attempting few landings, except in the company of some member of the Mission.

It is remarkable, after what I have stated, that it was on Santa Cruz that the Spaniards attempted to plant their first colony. In 1597, Mendana actually commenced the erection of buildings at Graciosa Bay; his project failed, and it was near these shores that the chief of the expedition expired. It was in this group also that La Perouse was lost with all his ships—at Vanikoro. In these waters D'Entrecasteaux died. It was on Santa Cruz that Commodore Goodenough was killed; and all the deaths by violence, without exception, which have occurred in the Mission have been occasioned by the natives of this group, from Bishop Patteson to Edwin Nobbs and Fisher Young—five or six in number. Conscious of these facts, it was with the keenest interest that one morning we sighted the distant islands of Vanikoro and Tupoua, and hoped, ere evening came, to meet the natives on Santa Cruz. These islands lie nearly north of the Torres group. The most southerly is Vanikoro, at present untouched by the Mission, full of natives wild and dangerous in disposition. It lies so far away from the next island that it would, in my opinion, need a clergyman to itself. No boy has ever yet been obtained from it; and remembering the delicacy of their constitution when taken from their homes, the problem is a difficult one. Northward again lies Tupoua, itself scarcely any better known than Vanikoro. It is forty miles distant from what is called the island of Santa Cruz, where our Mission is strongest. Mr. Forrest, in charge of Santa Cruz at present, has made one journey thither in his boat. But his native crew were nervous all the time that he was ashore, and would not leave him for an instant, fearful of the excitable and changeable nature of the people. Forty miles north of Tupoua the island of Santa Cruz is reached. Its southern shore has never yet been visited by white men so far as we know. There would appear to be some good anchorages for ships inside little islands and reefs; and one of these islands, named after Lord Howe, seems especially to act as a breakwater. Santa Cruz itself is some twenty miles by ten in width, with a range of hills in the centre, which acts as a watershed. Two facts regarding this southern shore are worthy of notice. The eye catches no glimpse of cocoanut palms. The people are so often at war with each other that it is of little use planting these trees, since they would be soon destroyed. The natives on this side also have no canoes. The Reef islands, which form a semicircle in these seas, are all on the northern side, and men who wish to visit them walk across the islands and embark in canoes from this northern shore; they never paddle from the southern side. The middle of Santa Cruz is inhabited by a community which, though it may be of the same race, is distinguished by a great difference of occupation. These bush people, of course, build no canoes, but they make all the arrows, and sell them to the dwellers on the shores. They inhabit villages strongly defended, I am informed, and besides the manufacture of arrows they are also, I believe, the weavers of the only money current in Santa Cruz—the famous "feather money" made in coils, with a ground work of some fibre, and clothed with a covering of red feathers taken from the breast of a little bird. Nowhere else is this money known; and, most strange fact of all, I am assured by Mr. Forrest that this money has only come into existence during the last thirty years, within the memory, that is, of living persons. This is certainly an astonishing fact, when it is remembered that these native races appear to be strongly and immovably conservative in their habits. Santa Cruz is very thickly inhabited. Nowhere else did I see so many villages. They lie almost in consecutive rows along the shores in some places, and instead of being a mere collection of a few huts, the Cruzian villages are regular warrens; paths wind about a maze of dwellings until the visitor almost loses his bearings. From what I have already stated, it will be easily understood how great is the yearning in the Mission to get a strong hold over these people. Yet if the boys and girls cannot be taken to Norfolk Island in large numbers, it is difficult to see any solution of the problem. Is it possible that here, in this particular group, the plan of the Mission will have in the future to be modified? Will the school for the training of the future teachers and native Cruzian clergy have to be planted in the group itself? This means a large increase in the English staff, and a dislocation of previous methods. The language, to my untutored ear, seemed a dreadful one. It sounded much more like the jabbering of a monkey than that of any other spot. It seemed to be the correct thing to clip every word, and to pronounce the rest of it at the back of the throat with little, if any, use of the lips. This is partly owing, no doubt, to the free use of betel nut, which keeps the mouth full of saliva, and prevents here, at least, any very definite pronunciation. At the same time this is but a poor and inadequate reason, for, in the Solomons, where every one is also a betel chewer, we come to a most graceful and melodious language. Santa Cruz was the one spot where I felt that it would be useless for me to attempt to read the service of Confirmation in the native tongue. There is one sad fact in the life of the Cruzians. They treat their women as beasts of burden. Nowhere else in Melanesia did I notice the degradation of the women as in this spot. They were never seen with the men, but kept to themselves entirely; and if any of them passed a man they were compelled to turn their backs or throw a covering over their faces. Here also the women do all the hard work in the yam gardens and carry the loads, while the men do the weaving with the looms. The women looked broken down and degraded, whilst the men are noted for their magnificent bearing and fine physique. Nowhere else did I see such finely-developed specimens of humanity, such chests and shoulders and legs, as among the Cruzian men. A Santa Cruz man with his powerful bow and heavy arrows (four feet long) is a splendid sight; and they are fearless fighters. They never skulk behind the trees, but as soon as their excitable natures catch fire they rush into the open and fight grandly. Many a time Mr. Forrest has run out and stood between two parties of angry natives, determined to check the whistling arrows and to make peace; and as a fine has to be paid for every arrow that is fired before a truce can be made, it is of the utmost importance to intervene at the earliest possible moment. Sometimes this intrepid gentleman has walked backwards and forwards between the hostile parties till midnight, determined that peace should be made, and giving them no rest till all the details were satisfactorily settled. Meanwhile the women, before they go to their long day's work in the gardens, have to cook their husbands' food; and at night, ere they eat anything themselves, they have to cook the evening meal for these lords of creation. It is, indeed, most gratifying to know that in the vicinity of our schools a better way is coming into vogue. The men are learning to help their wives, and to apportion the common burden more equitably. Of course this is the case among the Christians themselves; but the effect of the convert's example is having its result upon those who live around. Thank God for this most practical effect of "the new teaching." I trust I have not wearied my readers by this somewhat lengthy introduction. Let me now introduce them in due form to the Santa Cruz natives, and describe the scene as it presented itself to me on the eventful day when I first sailed along these romantic shores. I have nothing special to say of the general appearance of the island. It was like any other South Sea coral-bound shore. But the people—how different they appeared!—so vivacious, so full of laughter and gesticulation. In some sense it was like the sensation experienced by a sober Englishman accustomed to the ponderous ways of his race, when he is landed upon the shores of the Emerald Isle and finds himself face to face with laughing Paddy, with his quick motions and voluble tongue.

Let us imagine that the *Southern Cross* has been sailing along the northern shore of Santa Cruz to get to her anchorage at Nelua. Even if the vessel be a good distance from the land, she will already have been hailed by several canoes laden with food and curiosities. The canoes are beautifully made, with a stout outrigger, and a sort of platform upon it for the goods. The occupants are probably two stalwart natives with enormous nose rings, a round white disc of shell, some eight inches in diameter, on their breasts, and a perfect collection of rings and beads as earrings in each ear. They will probably rise in their seats and shout vociferously as soon as they are near enough. When told that we shall anchor at Nelua, and if they have been paddling towards us, immediately the two men at the same moment reverse their positions and paddle the canoe in the opposite direction, determined, come what may, to be the first on board still. Hardly has the ship anchored before we are in the midst of a scene that cannot be matched for interest and excitement. The decks swarm at once with excited men so delighted to see the captain and clergy again, that they are all jabbering at once—there is no other word for it—and what a strange and wonderful spectacle they present! The first man who stepped on board reminded me of one of the beaux of Charles II.'s time, making allowance for the scanty clothing! He had a closely-cropped head, powdered carefully with white lime, making his hair look like a well-kept wig. His frank and hearty bearing, full of confidence, and his face beaming with joy, made one *en rapport* with this untutored Melanesian at once. He had, of course, his disc of white shell on his chest, his multitudinous earrings and large nose-ring, and his hands held his bow and arrows—arrows that Romilly has called puny. But there could not be a greater mistake. They are heavier than the English arrow, considerably more than a yard long, and tipped with human bone, worked to a point so fine that a broken fragment left in the wound would remain, and cause tetanus. But there is still one more decoration to be noticed. The young children, as well as the men and women, carry a bag containing pepper leaf, areca nut, and lime in a dried gourd. The effect upon the mouth is hideous beyond words. It makes it a cavern full of black teeth, with the lips exuding a red juice. If my readers can imagine such a mouth vociferating, laughing, and talking as fast as it can, and then multiply such a figure by fifty or sixty, he will get some idea of the deck of the *Southern Cross* when she anchors at Santa Cruz. My "buck," whom I have described, began by walking up to the captain and poking him in the ribs and patting his back and pulling his beard in the greatest good-humour and in the highest of spirits. The day was when an embrace followed in order to rub noses, the effect being a closer acquaintance with that terrible mouth than was pleasant. Hand-shaking has now taken the place of the old salute, to the relief of the English. Then commences a period of bargaining. The crew, the captain, the clergy, all have to buy something in return for tobacco. Nor are there any shrewder men at a bargain than the Cruzians. As some one has said, "Whatever a Cruzian does not know about this form of traffic is not worth knowing."

But let us suppose that the ship has only anchored for an hour or so. The time soon comes to clear the ship. The anchor is on board, the canoes alongside are full of shouting men, holding out articles yet unsold. On board the commotion and excitement wax greater and greater; some are calling for their canoes, some are making a last bargain. At length the majority push off, for the ship is at last in motion. Still a few remain on board. One of these lowers himself into the water, and as he takes the plunge he holds his possessions up above his head in his left hand, his body disappears, but rises again ere the water reaches that left wrist. The last who remain stand on the bulwarks, and with a wild shout leap overboard and swim off with peals of laughter to their friends in the canoes. I have tried to draw this picture of the arrival at Santa Cruz because it affords a good illustration of the characteristic qualities of this race.

The general history of the Mission in this centre is as follows: The earliest landings by Bishop Patteson seem to have been in 1862, but no boys were obtained. It was in these days that Wadrokal, a native deacon, began work in the group, but not till some years later. In 1864 the bishop was in Graciosa Bay, when his boat was fired upon by the natives. The reason for it was a feeling of suspicion on the part of the people. They could not understand why the white men had come. The bishop escaped unhurt, but two young men, Norfolk Islanders, bearing historic names, Edwin Nobbs and Fisher Young, who had joined the Mission, were wounded, and died of tetanus. This sad occurrence prevented any further landing for some years. But two years afterwards, in 1866, while Captain Tilly was taking soundings in the ship, canoes came off to ask whether the men who had been wounded were alive or dead. On September 20, 1871, Bishop Patteson was murdered at Nukapu. In 1875 Commodore Goodenough died of wounds received at Carlisle Bay. In 1883 two hundred people were taken away by labour vessels, but the results were so tragic to the labourers that all recruiting in this group was stopped by the English Government. In 1884 the memorial cross standing at Nukapu was erected. In 1888 a similar cross was put up in Carlisle Bay to the memory of Commodore Goodenough. I shall refer again to many of these events in their proper places.

I believe the first real hold over the people by the Mission was gained, under God, by the restoration to their own island of two Reef Islanders by Bishop Selwyn, in 1877. These men had been blown away from their home in a strong sea-breeze, and had landed on Malcita, in the Solomons. The thrilling story of their escape will be related in due time.

Mr. Forrest before his House at Nelua, Santa Cruz. Feather Money to buy a Wife for a Teacher.

CHAPTER XIII.

NELUA, IN SANTA CRUZ.

TO step ashore at Santa Cruz! To sleep among people so famed for outrages committed in moments of excitement! The very thought was inspiring. So it happened that on Sunday morning, October 2, 1892, I went ashore with Mr. Forrest and the clergy. We had already had our excitements. From Te Motu a canoe had paddled out, longing to sell something. When near the ship, which would not stop, the two natives stood up to vociferate. At the same instant the outrigger gave way, and the men disappeared among the waves, appearing again with such a rueful look on their faces that they were greeted with a roar of laughter from our deck. Then, on anchoring, Forrest came off in a canoe, looking considerably battered. It was not wonderful, indeed, for a few days before he had nearly lost his life. The canoe he was in upset some miles out at sea, and for hours they were trying in vain to right it. To make matters worse, a big fish with a sword-like proboscis came under them, and would not depart. The two natives, by way of comfort, told Forrest that a wound from this fish produced tetanus infallibly. At length they were sighted from the shore and rescued.

Our first act ashore was a service, then a Confirmation and a celebration of Holy Communion. To see a church full of Cruzians was in itself a wonderful fact. The school and the church stand close together. On one side is the dancing ground, on the other Forrest's own house. Hard by flows a river of fresh water, affording capital bathing, and this privilege the natives utilize to the full. I suppose that every one bathes daily, the sexes each having a special spot. One of the comical adventures the next day was the mode of taking the bath as it obtains in this spot. We undressed in Mr. Forrest's house, putting on what we may call "native costume," then we proceeded to march through the village to the water, followed by an eager crowd of men, women, and children, who wished to see the bishop and the clergy take headers. They were gratified to their hearts' content, and then we ran back and exchanged native for English attire.

The most prominent character at Nelua is Natei, the chief. I met three chiefs during my voyage, who impressed me with their strong personality: Soga, in Ysabel, who is now a devout Christian; Takdi, in Cristoval, still a heathen, but well affected; and Natei, at Santa Cruz, a heathen, and scarcely to be called a well-affected person. The latter is a very powerful man, every inch a chief in appearance, with a fine physique. He carries himself in a dignified manner, and when he is standing, armed with bow and arrows in picturesque native dress, no one could fail to be struck with his appearance. He is a dead shot, and has done many a cruel and ruthless deed, and is a bad husband. A short while ago one of his seven wives hanged herself, to end a life of misery. Of late his power has been waning. A village named Taape, a few miles off, has accepted a school in place of being at Natei's beck and call to oppose the Christians. Three times has Natei renounced his ghosts, but again the old Adam asserts itself, and he begins to repair his ghost-house. On the Monday morning (October 3)—a day never to be forgotten, for I can never hope to spend a birthday in so romantic a manner again—we went to pay the chief a visit of state. From the courtyard of his house the *Southern Cross* could be seen anchored in the distance, and surrounded by canoes, who had been there since four a.m., waiting patiently for customers. On Sundays they know that buying is not permitted. Our visit began by our squeezing ourselves through a very narrow and low door into a fine house some forty feet square, and lofty also. Here Natei's men live, and here guests are entertained. I was given a place of honour on a clean mat. Welchman, with a touch of fever on him, laid himself down on his back and tried to be oblivious of the world generally. I had previously been initiated into Cruzian etiquette, therefore I was not surprised when, after an attempt to talk which failed dismally, Natei left the room, but returned almost immediately with some good mats under his arm. These he threw down before me in silence, according to the best form of polite society among his people, and resumed his seat. Now, it would be transgressing every rule of manners to say "Thank you," or to appear pleased. The right course is to look at the things gravely, and to appraise their value coolly without undue signs of pleasure. This I accomplished after the manner of a courtier well versed in *la haute politesse*. It was now my turn. From my trade-bag I extracted twenty sticks of tobacco, two fathoms of calico, twelve pipes (not meerschaums), two knives, etc., and threw them elegantly before the chief. With extraordinary good manners, he also paid no attention to the gift, but clearly was content. All this time dusky warriors, clustered round, were watching the actions of the great unknown bishop and the mighty chief of Nelua. In a few minutes we requested leave to see the dilapidated ghost-house. It was a curious place, spacious, and painted all over; that is to say, all the wooden beams had devices in red and figures not unlike Egyptian paintings, only much ruder. In the centre of the house there stood a row of poles cut at the top until they might have passed for bed-posts, and some six feet high. Two of these, in place of standing upright, were in a horizontal position. These posts are supposed to be figurative of ancestors. I think I heard that they had names, but no one seemed to understand why two occupied a position differing from the rest. Natives are not fond of talking of their old faith when they give it up, and the unconverted are equally reticent. Behind the posts, which were about eight in number, I think, there were pens made of bamboo, some five feet long and two or three wide, not unlike little pigsties, with sides two or three feet high. There was nothing in them, but I was given to understand that they were receptacles for food. These gifts were presented possibly not to ancestors so much as to spirits which were never in man, but are possessed of power. The subject, however, of the Cruzian's old religion seems at present wrapped in mystery. Mr. Forrest is the best authority, but he does not claim to know much yet of which he can speak with certainty. To turn from old Natei, with his cruel face and his ill-treated wives, to Natei's sweet-looking daughter is a wonderful step. She is a Christian, her baptismal name being Monica. Let those who wish to see the power of the Divine Spirit experience what I saw here. It is difficult, nay, impossible, to describe the change from heathenism in a bad form to a sweet Christian gentleness. Monica is married to "James Goodenough." It is startling to hear the name, and to be introduced to a stalwart Cruzian, one of the teachers at Nelua. I confirmed these two; nor can there be any doubt that, in a few years, a great change will come over Nelua and its neighbourhood. With Natei gone, and Monica's influence predominant, and James as teacher, the old ghost-house will disappear, and the people will be tamed. The customs of Santa Cruz do not permit a son-in-law to speak direct to his father-in-law; if he meets him he does not see him. A short time before I was there Natei was in his daughter's house, and James, standing near, wished to communicate with him. What could he do? A boy was brought in. James spoke to the boy, and the boy repeated it to Natei. Natei answered the boy, and the lad repeated the words to James, though all three were standing within a yard of each other.

The following story will illustrate some of the difficulties which come in the way of a native Christian. There is a teacher at Nelua named Robert. His brother died a few years ago, leaving a wife. They were both heathens. Now, by native law it was Robert's duty to marry his brother's widow, but Robert was already married, and when called upon to fulfil his duty he refused; he could not act otherwise. One day Robert was passing along the track, and the widow, supposing that he, as a Christian, would not adhere to strict native custom, called out his name. But for any woman to call out any man's name is a heinous offence. As it happened, a man overheard her, and immediately he raised his bow and shot her in the leg, and the poor woman died of tetanus ten days afterwards. The people now came to Robert and accused him of being the cause of the woman's death, and declared he must pay the fine. Acting under Forrest's advice, he paid it, but he had to sell everything he had in the world to raise the money.

I should mention that the origin of the ghost-houses on this northern shore of Santa Cruz is somewhat mysterious. They are not used by the bush people, nor by those who live on the southern shore. Mr. Forrest believes that the system has been introduced from the Reef Islands, which are inhabited by a different race in part, some being Polynesians. As one stands on the shore at Nelua, with the large canoes drawn up, capable of going distances of a hundred miles, with a deck-house to live in, a grand cone-shaped mountain stands up out of the sea some ten miles distant. This is Tinakula, a volcano still active. I saw thin columns of smoke ascending from the peak. Twenty years ago it was very active, and it is likely that some day it may burst out again. The Cruzians do not live on its slopes, but they have gardens there, and often sail across to work in them. I feel inclined to linger yet awhile over Nelua. I cannot forget the pile of mats, dancing clubs, arrows, etc., with which I was presented as a birthday present by Forrest, nor the exertions this same kind friend made to provide a birthday feast; the kitchen looked, as we laughingly said, like some north-country smelting works, with dusky figures, more or less unclothed, flitting before the fires. I cannot forget the solemn consecration of the churchyard, when, as we traced its borders in procession, singing hymns the while, we were watched with grave curiosity by Natei and a band of warriors, who had first been giving a dance in honour of myself. I cannot forget, last but not least, how-now at length a spot of light, real and bright, burns on these shores, on which Patteson longed to plant the Cross, but was always baffled. In 1871 he says that for nine years running he had tried to land here, but had failed. In 1862, however, he had been ashore in seven places in one day, and had met one thousand two hundred natives, according to his calculation. After this their suspicions were roused by the heartless cruelty of labour vessels, and his work was checked. The first Bishop Selwyn had rowed several times into Graciosa Bay, but had never landed. Now the school is firmly planted, and I was able to sleep ashore in perfect safety. I remember how on that night I lay awake with sleeping Cruzians on the floor round me as I mused on the ways of God, and how in His own good time He makes His name known. The conquest of Santa Cruz has begun; but "how shall they hear except they be sent?" Who shall send but we who bear Christ's name, and are pledged to His service?

In 1895 Mr. Forrest had a terrible experience at Nelua. Early in the year the natives affirmed that the ship had brought influenza. There were many deaths, and the natives were furious, and turned upon Forrest's Christians as the cause of the malady. During Holy Week the school premises were besieged. One morning

Forrest found a poisoned arrow in his curtain; it had penetrated the side of the house. During service for weeks a guard had to be kept, and throughout the night as well. Hearing one day that a force was advancing against him, Forrest stole into the bush with a party of armed natives, and suddenly appeared in the path behind the attacking force, thus placing them between two fires. The enemy thereupon retired; and the admiral of the Australian station (Cyprian Bridge), who visited Santa Cruz, warmly congratulated Forrest on achieving a victory without bloodshed. The position amongst these excitable people has been made more complicated by the visits of French labour vessels. The returned labourers from Noumea seem to have learnt nothing but evil among Europeans. One of these labourers fired at Forrest with a rifle. This gallant man refused to leave his people, and held on his solitary way, fearing nothing, quite determined to win his way in God's name.

THE ISLAND OF TE MOTU.

A few miles to the west of Nelua there is a bay with a good anchorage. It bears a historic name, for this is Graciosa Bay, where the Spaniards, in 1597, under Mendana, attempted to settle their colony, but without success. They mention that the natives live in round huts like beehives. And it is an example of the conservatism of natives that here, at Te Motu, the island at the mouth of Graciosa Bay, the huts are round still. Nowhere else does this habit attain but here; here the custom has held its ground for three hundred years and more. Strange to say, however, a round hut was almost the first I saw in the South Seas. My first landing-place was at Maré, in the Loyalty Group. We called at Nengone to pay a pension to the Rev. M. Wadrokal. This deacon of ours had been stationed at Santa Cruz years ago, and had built himself a Te Motu hut in this spot. I was amazed at the clustering villages in Te Motu. The people seemed to swarm, and the huts were built so close together that one quite lost one's bearings in the winding paths. These people are most excitable. Many a thrilling moment has Mr. Forrest had in this island. Perhaps he was never in greater danger than when he landed unwittingly on a spot which had been "tapued." As he walked up the familiar path he was met by a raging mob of men, with arrows drawn to the head, and much too angry to explain their desires distinctly. Nothing but cool pluck saved him, and by the evening he had calmed down their passions. I believe that, with a delightful audacity, he abused them roundly for their stupidity. This step, coupled with perfect fearlessness, saved his life. My own landing was intensely interesting. There is no shelving shore here, nothing but a jagged edge of coral rock, with a flat surface shoreward, and a precipitous descent at the edge of the reef. The surf was alternately boiling over the reef, rushing up over the surface, and retreating so as to leave uncovered the line of coral. We had to wait on our oars until the signal was given, and then with a spurt we rode on the top of a wave right over the edge till we were landed on the reef, where the boat was seized by twenty willing friends, and dragged further up before the wave retired. Our return was still more exciting, for we all had to get into the boat and pull for dear life, so as to escape being left on the cruel edge of the reef if we were a few seconds too late in our effort.

All, however, was safely accomplished, and camera and plates, bishop and clergy, were brought back to the ship, after having been broiled under a sun so hot that I still remember the sensation. The school at Te Motu is not so firmly established as that at Nelua, but the foothold has been secured, and one of the finest churches in Melanesia now stands among the round huts. It was near this place that Edwin Nobbs and Fisher Young were killed. Patteson had been ashore, but upon his return the suspicions of the natives were roused, and they began firing into the boat. The bishop was in the stern. Holding the rudder in his hand, he tried to ward off the arrows, but on looking round he discovered that these poor fellows had been wounded, though Atkin had escaped. The deaths of these two devoted men gave the bishop a great shock, and there are some who think that he was never the same man afterwards. Nobbs and Young were the only Norfolk Islanders (ex-Pitcairners) who ever joined the Mission. Nobbs was, of course, the son of the well-known clergyman and chaplain. Two years afterwards some canoes paddled out to the *Southern Cross* as Captain Tilley was taking observations near Te Motu, and the men in them inquired whether any of those upon whom they had fired had died from their wounds.

CHAPTER XIV.

TAAPE, IN SANTA CRUZ.

SOME four miles east of Nelua there is a village which formerly supplied warriors to Natei for his raids and when he wished to annoy the school people. But the war—the Christian war—has been carried into the enemy's camp. Natei has been deserted by this village, and they asked and obtained a school. It was obvious that the *Southern Cross* should touch here, and that a strange bishop ought to assist to make as much as possible of the public demonstration in favour of the new movement. Before we landed Forrest said to me, "You may be sure old Natei will not be absent to-day. He will wish to know whether the chief here is to get as big a present as he." It was a true forecast. In due time, as I sat on the mat of honour in the palace of Taape, I noted Natei peering round the corner of the entrance with a look of anxious jealousy on his face. And now commenced one of the most amusing experiences of the voyage. The same formalities were observed as at Nelua. The chief gave me mats, though not of a superior quality. I in return presented nearly as much as I had given Natei. The effect, however, was startling. Apparently far more had been given by me than had been expected, and the chief was guilty of a breach of good manners. He burst into a loud laugh, unable to control his feelings. Upon this a spirit of mischief seized me, and I gave him more tobacco. Again he laughed, and going away a second time he brought me a fresh mat. More tobacco followed, and of course the excitement increased. In the recesses of the hut, behind their lord and master, were seated the four wives, who were eagerly watching the proceeding. But now their desire for the herb that cheers broke through the rules of good Cruzian society, and I was conscious of a shower of mats following around me, discharged over the head of the chief, and for the benefit of the man who possessed such tobacco. What could I do but return the compliment by a discharge of tobacco-sticks at the ladies? I did so, and with shouts of laughter I was once more greeted with the shower of mats, and once more it was returned by what their souls loved. I was conscious soon that I should be unable to carry off my booty, and I turned to Forrest in despair. The mound of mats seemed to be several feet high, and it was time to retreat. Then came the climax. The chief exclaimed, "I will give him a pig." Then we fled, convinced that the Church had been strongly founded in Taape, though in a manner unexpected by a band of sober-minded clergymen. I believe the pig was duly brought on board. But my last memories of Taape bring back to me the picture of a bishop staggering down to the boat, carrying a vast pile of mats, and held by the hand at the same time by the lord of that country. Natei had disappeared, filled, no doubt, with envy, and coveting some of the material wealth of the ship. The chief of Taape accompanied us to the ship in his canoe, and as I was waving a last farewell to the kind old man from the deck, he seized the bow by his side and hurled it on board as a last act of hospitality to one who is not likely to forget that particular spot in Santa Cruz, nor the welcome he received there. The bow in question hangs in the hall of my home, and the mats now form a dado round the walls of the little extemporized chapel at Bishopscourt, in Tasmania. The latest news from the Mission is that the chief of Taape has been too much intimidated to help the good cause. Moreover, the first teacher had been too weak a man.

CARLISLE BAY, IN SANTA CRUZ.

A few miles further east, and only some six from Nelua, there is a little harbour formed by an island and a coral reef. Though a mile of open surface is stretched out, calm and inviting looking as an anchorage, there is not really any great extent of deep water, not more perhaps than sufficient to permit one large ship to swing at anchor. The scorching heat of the sun upon the day when we anchored here I shall always remember, as well as the cool and peaceful evening when our work was done, and we chatted quietly on deck under the stars, with Melanesians sleeping round us, and, in the distance, the cross in memory of Commodore Goodenough standing close by the water's edge. There are no Christians yet in the village by the bay; the people are really Reef Islanders, who have come over to settle, and there is constant communication between them and their kinsfolk. The name of the village is a long one,

L.

Matalianielovla. It is the spot which possesses a painful interest on account of the attack on the Commodore. By nature the people are excitable, so much so that Forrest did not recommend any one to go ashore but the clergy and a few Cruzian boys. The natives could not be relied upon if we did anything which offended them through ignorance of their customs. Indeed when it was suggested that we should take a photograph of the cross from a boat, it was thought wise to go ashore first, and tell them what we were about. The sight of a white man gazing intently at them through a box with a small hole in it would have given fair occasion for suspicion until some explanation had been afforded. We were welcomed most cordially; all gathered before the camera, and soon we had the satisfaction of taking what proved to be the best photograph of the cross, and of the locality, that I have seen. The cross itself stands on a sort of raised platform close to the water's edge. Within thirty yards of it is the little beach where all land; and at this spot we induced the natives to collect in order to obtain, so far as we could, a realistic representation of the scene when the Commodore was there. It appears to be certain that the death of one of the most gallant and noble minded of men was caused by ignorance of native customs. Goodenough did what any Englishman would have done guided by the ways of his own country, but which, from a native's point of view, was unfortunate. Like any one animated by the desire to be friendly, he landed at this spot and was received (as we were) in a most friendly manner. Then, having spent some time with them, he determined to visit the next village. What could be more natural? Yet no step could here have been more fatal. Villages

Commodore Goodenough's Cross, Santa Cruz.

situated as these two were are often at war. To approach one of them from the other is therefore to come from the enemy's land, and therefore as a person to be resisted. It happened that these two places had been at war for years. Had Commodore Goodenough and his party reached the other village they would probably have fared badly, coming as he did from a suspicious quarter. As it happened I believe they went only half way, and then retraced their steps. But the mistake had been made, and his old friends had now become suspicious, nay, hostile. He was returning from the enemy's quarter. The result was that the arrows were discharged, and one of the men we could least afford to lose was killed. Had one of our clergy been with him, he would have been told to get into his boat after concluding his visit, and, having put out to sea, to have landed again at the next village without saying where he had been before. The record of his last days should be read by all who value Christian heroism coupled with resignation at the certain approach of a terrible death. I remember that Dean Stanley used to say that the death of Commodore Goodenough was one of the most striking he had ever heard of. The chivalrous desire to help the natives, the command not to return their fire, his speech to his men when death was certain, the scene upon the deck of a man-of-war, all tended to make it unique. To me the day when we stood under his cross, and the evening when we prayed to be made as true and faithful to duty as he was, will never be forgotten. My readers will be glad to know that the two villages are now at peace. They adopted, I believe, a custom common here, namely, the planting of a young cocoanut palm, with a resolution that when it bore fruit all ill-will should cease. As the tree takes seven years to bear fruit, it will easily be understood that there is plenty of time in which to pay off old scores before the day of peace dawns. I am not sure, indeed, whether in this case some one did not cut down the first tree so planted because some outstanding grievance had not been avenged. At all events the second tree grew, and the old hatred ceased. I do not know what the natives of this village with the unpronounceable name really think of the cross, whether for them it is a charm, but they take the greatest care of it, and are pleased when notice is taken of it. It was a strange thing to note that not more than fifteen yards from it a new ghost house was being erected. But if only adequate attention could be given to Santa Cruz by the Mission, the cross will win the day.

THE REEF ISLANDS.

The contrast is great indeed between the Reef Islands and those we have just left. It is like passing from Vanua Lava, in the Banks Group, to Rowa. There are no high hills, or long slopes watered by streams in these Reef Islands. Their name indicates what they are—low flat patches, surrounded by coral reefs, extending far out into the sea. The captain showed me one which stretched for thirteen miles under the surface with water on it so shallow that he could not cross it, an awkward place on a dark and squally night. These islands form a sort of semicircle, some twenty miles distant from Santa Cruz, on the north and east. I do not know how many there are, but the names of seven, which are inhabited, I know—Nakapu, Nufiloli, Pileni, Matima, Lomlom, Nipua, and Netuna. Beyond these again there lies the Duff Group, only just touched by us through the enterprise of Mr. Forrest. The first school has now been started. These islands alone would more than tax the strength of a white superintending clergyman, but at present they are treated as the rim of a sphere which is far larger and entirely beyond the compass of any man. I landed upon two only of these islands—Pileni and Nukapu.

PILENI.

Those who are learned in ethnology assert that the natives in Pileni and in most of this group are Polynesians. From these places the ghost houses seem to have been introduced into Santa Cruz. One striking difference between the people no one could help marking. In Santa Cruz, more than anywhere else, the women are drudges, and never consort with the men in public. In Pileni I saw an intercourse so free and untrammelled that I was fairly amazed. We went so soon as we had landed into the men's house, or what answers to the gamal in the Banks Islands, and to our surprise the women and girls came freely in and out and were unreproved. As we sat there that afternoon, in the great heat, leaning back and chatting, and buying a few of the island products, I could not help recalling the manner in which Bishop Patteson was killed only a few miles away. Just as in his case, so here, there were crowds of natives present, and behind us a row of them had squeezed themselves in between the wall and ourselves. It was a man sitting thus behind the bishop who struck the fatal blow.

Pileni, like any other recently formed coral island, consists of a more or less circular space but little raised above the sea, planted with cocoanuts among the usual bush, and supporting a small population. There was rejoicing to-day among the clergy, because they had been promised a boy to be taken to Norfolk Island. The parting between the lad and his relatives was affecting, proving, I think, the affectionate nature of their disposition, and the reality of their family life. One after another the women seized him and kissed him, whilst the men rubbed noses. As to his mother, after she had bade him farewell "she lifted up her voice and wept." There is no better phrase to express her action; and in this she was followed by her women friends, until the air was filled by a really great volume of sound, whilst they swung their bodies about, and showed signs of being distracted with grief. The boy himself was crying, but he tried his best to look unconcerned. I believe there is a bright future here for our mission. There is no school as yet, nor do I suppose there are any baptized persons. We soon returned to the ship, and then made our way to an island with a name known to all who read these lines—Nukapu.

NUKAPU.

The interest of Nukapu will ever be, of course, centred round the death of Bishop Patteson at this spot on September 20, 1871. It was here that a life was ended by violence which will ever be precious, both in its achievements and in its ending, to the universal Church. Let us dwell lovingly over a few of the striking incidents of his life ere we come to the day of his death. As a lad he was very much struck with the Absolution in our Church service. He longed to say it, he said, because it made people so happy. As a boy at Eton he was saved from death, or at least some

Bishop Patteson.

P. 150.

serious injury, by the queen, then a girl. At Eton
Montem he was running beside the royal carriage
and stumbled, and would have fallen under the
wheels had not the young queen seized him by
his hand. How much depended upon that happy
movement! In 1854 a sermon of Bishop Selwyn
won him to work in the South Seas. Then we
hear of him at Kohimarama with thirty-eight
scholars, speaking thirteen dialects or languages.
There he sits surrounded with his dear lads, one
of whom has given him a new word, and at once
he is hunting it up Melanesia and down Polynesia,
till the root is found among the Malays. Then
the scene changes, and he is on a coral island in
a narrow path, and meets a native with arrow on
the string and bow drawn tight. "Shoot away!"
shouted Patteson, "it is all right," and his pluck
and his smile disarm his opponent. And anon he
is in a boat, and, when fifty yards off the shore, he
jumps into the water and swims to land with a
little book in the crown of his hat for new words,
and presents tied round his neck. Then came the
day when he was consecrated first Bishop of Melanesia. Three Eton bishops had met to consecrate
a fourth. Utabilava (not Henry Tagalana, as Miss
Yonge says) held the prayer-book for Bishop
Selwyn while the words of consecration were being
uttered. Listen also to Selwyn's words, they are
brimful of feeling: "He will go forth to sow beside
many waters, to cultivate an unknown field, himself
unknown, and speaking in the name of an unknown
God. . . . He will have to persuade them by the
language of signs to give up their children to his
care, and while he teaches them the simplest
elements which are taught in an infant school, to
learn from them a new language for every island.
. . . So may every step of thy life, dear brother,

be in company with the Lord Jesus. May Christ be with thee as a light to lighten the Gentiles. . . . May He be with you when you go forth to those mingled races who still show forth the curse of Babel and wait for the coming of a second Pentecost." Then, soon, Patteson is to be seen as a nurse in days never to be forgotten, when at Kohimarama fifty-two out of sixty scholars were attacked with dysentery, and only six died, because the bishop and his clergy became nurses night and day. But turn to this very group, Santa Cruz, of which we are speaking: For nine years running he tried to land, and could not. In 1864, Edwin Nobbs, and Fisher Young were killed, though Patteson tried to shield them from the arrows. Some one says, "He was never the same again after their death." So we come to the year 1871. He had been very ill at Norfolk Island, and those who knew him best said they thought he could not live long. Mota that year gave him nearly three hundred baptized members. This was the greatest cheer. Then the ship bore him to the Solomons; there he heard of a labour vessel (was it the *Emma Bell?*), which made no secret that it was going to Santa Cruz, and the captain meant to get labour by fair means or foul. Slowly against a head wind the *Southern Cross* beat back to Santa Cruz. The wind fell light, but was right ahead; they could make no progress. For a long time they were almost stationary near Tinakula, that volcano close to the Reef Islands; it was in full activity. The night before his death (on September 19) he was reading the hundred and fourth Psalm, and looked up to the fiery discharges and clouds of steam as he came to the words, " If He do but touch the mountains they shall smoke."

Let us hear now the words of one who was on

board. "In proportion as our weariness increased (because of the head wind) his interest deepened, till at last he seemed to think of nothing else save these poor people for whom he began to pray without ceasing. As he sat in the cabin with shaded eyes, or walked the deck, he seemed to be absorbed in meditation and prayer. At night the volcano and the earnest prayer for Santa Cruz ; next day a light head wind. Still we held on—we so weary, he so calm, hopeful, and happy." Hear now his own words in his diary (dated September 16, 1871).

"On Monday we go to Nukapu. I am fully alive to the probability that some outrage has been committed here. The master of the vessel whom Atkin saw, did not deny his intention of taking away from these or from any other islands any men or boys he could induce to come on board. I am quite aware we may be exposed to considerable risk on this account. I trust that all may be well, and that if it be His will that any trouble should come upon us, dear Joseph Atkin, his father's and mother's only son, may be spared."

September 19.—"Here we are becalmed ; for three days we have scarcely made ten miles in the direction we want to go. It is not prudent to go near the large island unless we have a good breeze and can get away from the fleets of canoes, if we see reason for so doing. We may have a hundred and fifty canoes round us, and perhaps sixty or eighty strong men on deck, as we had last year, and this year we have good reason for fearing that labour vessels have been here seeking to take away men. Yesterday, being becalmed, a large canoe from Nupani to Santa Cruz came near us. It could not get away, and the *Southern Cross* could not get near it, so we went to it in our boat.... They knew my name directly, and were quite at ease the moment they were satisfied it was the bishop. I shall be thankful if this visit ends favourably. It seems so sad to leave this fine people year after year in ignorance and darkness; but He knows and cares for them more than we do."

Nukapu is smaller, I think, even than Pileni. Even in its crowded days it never contained more than a hundred people, and now no more than a changing population of thirty, as upon the day that I was there. It is surrounded by a barrier reef, which is often most difficult to pass. The surf beats fiercely on it, and though the natives, when the reef is covered, will make straight for it, and battle across in their light canoes, it is very different with a ship's whaleboat; and I have heard of a clergyman being dropped at nine p.m. in the darkness, on a night of rain and wind, to find the reef and to pass the night on it till the daylight enables him to proceed. Upon the occasion of my own visit the sun was nearly setting when we reached the cross, and the last beams were shining full on the monument to the beloved bishop. It stands on a bank, raised some seven feet above the water's edge, and directly behind it is the house where the murder was committed, in the corner of the house close by the cross. The actual erection of that day has been pulled down, but it was rebuilt again with the same timbers.

It was about noon on September 20, 1871, when the *Southern Cross* hove to off Nukapu, though at a distance of several miles. There were two clergymen on board besides the bishop—the Rev. Joseph Atkin and the Rev. Mr. Brooke. All remarked that no canoes pulled out to them as they usually did even if the ship were three or four miles away. But the bishop said it was probably because they were too far from the reef, and that he would go ashore. The boat was manned by Joseph Atkin, stroke; Stephen Taroniara, three; John, a man whom I met in 1892, two; and another, whose name I do not remember, rowed the bow oar. When they arrived at the barrier reef some canoes came to meet them, and there was nothing unusual about their manner. As the whaleboat could not cross the reef, the bishop got into the chief's canoe and went ashore alone, telling the boat to wait for him outside. Several canoes stayed with the boat and chatted with our people amicably. They asked where they came from, and were told one from New Zealand, another from Bauro, and so on. The men in the canoes seem to have waited till the bishop had landed on the island and had time to get into the house. Then suddenly they took their bows and arrows and shot at ten yards distance at the four men, calling out, "This is for the man from New Zealand!" "This for Bauro!" and so forth. As soon as this happened our people took up their oars and rowed away as fast as they could. Mr. Atkin had received an arrow in the shoulder, Stephen was struck by five arrows, John by one in the shoulder, and as for "bow," he threw himself into the bottom of the boat and remained there till all danger was past, and escaped unhurt. The after career of this last individual I have not been able to discover. Apparently he has been lost sight of for many years. The boat reached the ship at last, and the wounded men were lifted out. Stephen said as he came on board, "The bishop and I."

Let us follow the bishop ashore. We saw him

last in the chief's canoe crossing the reef, and at length landing on the beach. It seems that he went into the house of which I have spoken, and laid himself down flat on his back, with his head on a Santa Cruz pillow, and closed his eyes. The place was full of people. Behind him there sat a man who had in his hand a wooden mallet. With this he struck the bishop on the top of his head. Death was instantaneous. It is said that he did not even open his eyes. Then in due time they stripped him of his clothes, except his stockings, dragged him a few yards at least, and, wrapping him in a mat, they placed him in a canoe. Meanwhile on board the *Southern Cross* there was grief and perplexity. At about three p.m.—not before, for they had to attend to the wounded—Mr. Bongard, the mate of the vessel, called for volunteers, and took the boat through the reef— for by this time it was possible—and rowed up and down near the shore looking to see if there were any signs of the bishop. Mr. Atkin insisted on going back in the boat. When they turned round to row back on one of these occasions they saw two canoes come out from the shore at some distance. A man in one of them seemed to anchor it with the help of a stone, then he jumped into the other canoe and the men paddled ashore again. Mr. Bongard made for the anchored canoe, and as they approached it they knew what was in it by a sight of the striped stockings. They found the body wrapped in a mat, with a palm branch on it, the fronds being tied into five knots. The top of the head was battered to pieces as if by a blunt instrument. There was no other wound except what looked like an arrow wound in the palm of the hand. It is probable this was made after death, for it is the custom for the relatives of a murdered man to pierce with arrows the body of any one whom they have killed in revenge. As soon as the body had been lifted into the boat there suddenly appeared upon the beach the whole population of the island, numbering then about a hundred; they gave a yell, and then vanished again. When the *Southern Cross* was reached once again the ship stood off to the northward, and at seven o'clock next morning the bishop's body was committed to the deep with the prayers of the Church. A sort of coffin was improvised, in which they placed him. The wounded men were carefully tended; but as is well known Stephen and Joseph Atkin died, the latter on September 27, the former on the day after. They were buried at sea among the Banks Islands. Mr. Atkin showed the first signs of tetanus while reading the Communion office. Writing just after his wound, he said "Seeing people taken away when, as we think, they were almost necessary to do God's work on earth, makes one think that we often think and talk too much about Christian work. What God requires is Christian men. He does not need the work, only gives it to form and perfect the character of the men whom He sends to do it. If it be God's will that I am to die, I know He will enable you to bear it, and to bring good to you out of it."

It is certain that the bishop was killed because five men had been kidnapped by a labour vessel. The sequel to this tragedy is also remarkable. The five men were carried off to Fiji; here one of them died, but the other four stole a boat and made their way before the sea breeze as far as Tanna. When they saw the volcano they turned north, and in due time reached Nukapu once more. But they brought dysentery with them. The result was that about half the natives of Nukapu died of this (to them) mysterious malady. And naturally the survivors saw in this the hand of the God of the bishop. There is no spot where a white man is so safe at this moment as Nukapu. The other day Mr. Forrest was there ill of fever. The inhabitants came to him, and after awhile their spokesman said, "Father, are you going to die?" Forrest, I believe, answered that he could not tell; they then said, "Because if you think you are going to die, will you go to the next island?"

The Mission after Patteson's death begged that no retaliatory measures should be taken by the Government, but it was without avail. H.M.S. *Rosario* burnt the village and bombarded the island. The result was that not until 1877 could the clergy touch here again. Bishop Selwyn came in that year with a Mr. Coote as a friend in addition to his staff. Mr. Coote has left an account of his feelings upon landing, and of the excitement he felt. On the memorial cross is the following inscription—

IN MEMORY OF

JOHN COLERIDGE PATTESON,

MISSIONARY BISHOP,

Whose life was here taken by men for whom he would gladly have given it. Sept. 20, 1871.

The effect of the bishop's death was tremendous. It was a fact noted in the Queen's speech to Parliament. It called attention to the unspeakable horrors of the then labour traffic; and I believe the worst abuses were brought to light and sternly repressed. In 1872 Dr. Codrington, the acting head of the Mission, wrote of the dreadful evils of the traffic and of the neglect of the Melanesians in Queensland. "I am persuaded," he said, "that

Bishop Patteson's Cross, Nukapu.

they might tell them of the existence of a God and of a Saviour and of a gospel of peace. This would at least remove the strange reproach that I have heard in the islands that Bishop Patteson was deceiving them about the importance of Christianity, for they heard nothing about it in Queensland. These Melanesians are still heathens, because they are carried into a Christian land, taken away from direct Christian teaching." Thank God this reproach is now being wiped away, but the neglect and the selfish cruelties of the past are an abiding blot on our English race. What a blush of shame rises in our faces when we think of the deeds of the English race in old days in America, in Africa, in Australia, and in the South Seas. How much we have to do to make reparation so far as reparation is possible.

We returned to the ship from Nukapu rather late in the evening. Then, after our evening meal, the bright moon rose, and the night was calm, as calm as on the eventful day in 1871. I do not forget our prayers, stimulated by the associations; then we found it hard to go to rest. Midnight found us still on deck talking and musing. The captain meanwhile had brought us to within a mile of Tinakula. The mountain was quiet, except for columns of steam from fissures at the top. And so Santa Cruz faded from my sight, but the memories remain. Bishop Selwyn called on the Church to "avenge" Patteson's death by giving Santa Cruz the gospel of peace. It is the true type of revenge, and I pray that those who read these lines may help to send aid to Mr. Forrest, who, single handed, is fighting our battle here in perils among waters, in perils among arrows, in perils among fever, and in loneliness.

CHAPTER XV.

THE SOLOMON ISLANDS.

IT is a well-known fact that travellers, looking back upon their experiences, remember most clearly the romance and not the discomforts. Memory sheds a golden haze over the past, adding a tender colouring to the whole landscape. I confess that it is so with myself, as I try to recall the Isles of Solomon. I suppose no white man would assert that they are desirable places for habitation, yet I find myself looking back fondly at the days I spent there, and wondering whether I shall ever have the happiness of seeing them again. From Santa Cruz the ship steers west to reach these abodes of wealth and bliss, as the Spaniards who discovered them in 1566 wished their people to believe. The tale of the coming of these first white discoverers has often been told. It will be sufficient to give the merest outline here. In 1566 Philip II. commissioned Mendana to sail from Callao for the purpose of annexing new lands to the Spanish crown. Mendana had for his pilot a gentleman named Gallego, who has left a full journal of the voyage, and a translation of it is to be found in Guppy's work on the Solomons. From this we discover that the expedition started on the day of St. Ysabel in 1566, and on the eightieth day afterwards, having only sighted land once in the interval, the Spaniards stepped ashore on an island which they named Ysabel. It is believed that the spot is a bay on the north-east side of the island, about the middle of it; and Mr. Woodford has tried to fix their wanderings in these regions in a paper read before the Geographical Society in England. The Spaniards also gave such names as Guadalcanar, Cristoval, Florida, and others. The journal of the pilot was not made public till this century; and the reason for its non-publication in the sixteenth century is alleged to be the fear that the name of Drake inspired. The Spaniards were apprehensive that if their new possessions were known to the famous Englishman, they would be playing into his hands. It is further stated that the name of the Isles of Solomon was given in order to induce the Spanish people to believe that the sources of King Solomon's wealth had at length been discovered, and lead to immigration into them. Gallego speaks of gold and silver among the natives; but it is impossible to guess what he could really have seen, for he appears to be a perfectly honest man, and yet the precious metals seem to be entirely absent from this region. Mendana many years afterwards died of fever near the Santa Cruz Group.

A traveller coming to the Solomons from the east at once realizes that he is approaching New Guinea. He will notice the cuscus, or opossum; crimson lories, white cockatoos and large hornbills will attract his attention, and though he will be glad to note the presence of beautiful rivers, he will also remember that crocodiles abound. None of these birds or beasts are known south or east of Cristoval, but they all belong to the fauna of New Guinea. Here is also a change in the weapons of the natives. In the Santa Cruz and in the Banks Islands we notice bows and arrows; but in the Solomons the common weapon is the spear. In Santa Cruz cannibalism is apparently unknown, in the Solomons it has been almost universal in past times, and is still fearfully common where the Mission work has not effected a change. A theory has sometimes been advanced that cannibalism has arisen from the want of other animal food, for which there has been a craving. But this theory is not supported by facts. There is, for instance, practically no difference between the island products of Santa Cruz and the Solomons —that is, pigs are the only four-footed animals for food, and they are abundant in both groups. Yet human flesh is regularly eaten in one group and never in the other. It seems to be more probable that the distinction between the two customs rests upon some religious belief which we have not yet fully detected. Speaking broadly, there is a very easy explanation of cannibalism in many of these islands. The belief that almost everything possesses mana, or power, is universal. In that case, if a man can eat his enemy, then his enemy's "mana" will be received into him. And in the Hebrides, a chief's portion of a man at a feast is the brain, the heart, and the feet. This view of cannibalism, in its origin at least, makes us view sympathetically, at all events, a custom which otherwise seems too horrible to be faced with anything but indiscriminating horror. Another striking feature in these islands is their size. At least six of them are close on a hundred miles in length, and some twenty or thirty in breadth. The mountains rise to heights of eight thousand feet, and in one case in Bougainville to ten thousand feet. Nothing, indeed, can be more beautiful than the aspect of Guadalcanar as the morning mists are floating away, with densely wooded slopes leading up to the masses of Mount Lammas, with broad reaches of fertile land near the shore, watered by deep rivers. Nor is the charm lessened by the fact that the traveller is gazing upon lands as little known as any in the world. No white man has ever penetrated far into the interior of Guadalcanar. No white man has ever been twenty yards from the shore in Maleita, anywhere except where our three schools are situated. Even labour vessels do not let their boats land, though they venture upon some of the rivers. To this romantic region let us now turn our attention, and see what the Mission has done in it. Without doubt the day has come when the demand for men and means of support for them in the Solomons and in Santa Cruz must be generously met if we are to do our duty in this region, where the Church of England is left to herself to do her work by the other religious bodies.

SAN CRISTOVAL.

Five schools ; sixty baptized ; a hundred and fifteen scholars ; two hundred and thirty attendants ; population unknown.

This, the first of this group that I visited, is a large island, some seventy miles long, and twenty in breadth. The first regular worker here was that devoted pioneer and afterwards martyr, the Rev. Joseph Atkin. The waves break on fringes of white coral sand, as elsewhere, yet there seemed to me to be a slight difference in the tropical foliage. The vegetation was more pleasing to the eye than, for instance, in the Banks Islands; and I came to see that the trees here stand out more distinctly, and possess more individuality because they are not so much shrouded with creepers, which further south give a somewhat sombre hue to many a tree-clad hillside. The mountains here rise to the height of some four thousand feet. I suppose that a few years ago all the inhabitants were addicted to cannibalism, and I should not like to guarantee that any village outside the Mission influence is free from it. The natives in the bush, and, indeed, by the seashore also, go often entirely unclothed; but the Mission, though it refuses to Anglicize its people, requires that degree of clothing which, from the Melanesian Mission point of view, is decent. Cannibalism, however, crops up in unexpected places. In 1892 one of the clergy had occasion to go ashore at Towatana late in the evening, and slept in the gamal, or men's quarters. This is the birthplace of Stephen Taroniara, who was one of the victims when Bishop Patteson was killed. There are no Christians now in this place; and I am not sure that there ever have been, with the exception of Stephen. Yet it was somewhat startling to the Rev. R. Comins to look up in the morning and see in the roof the remains of a human being. He called attention to the fact, and the natives began with shame to remove them. We cannot boast yet of the effect produced upon this island by the Mission. Five schools are all we have at present, and these are close together, all within sixteen miles on the north-west coast. I am not insensible to the degree of light which any heathen race may possess, but when wars and cannibalism and infanticide obtain everywhere, it is difficult not to use the strong language of the Psalmist, and think of abodes "full of darkness and cruel habitations." The school buildings I need not stay to describe. They are plain bamboo structures, with furniture of the simplest description—a plain table, a few books, a stand for a lamp of cocoanut oil, some benches—and you have the entire building and its contents. I asked the question once why all the school buildings were upon the shore, why none were inland. The answer gives an insight into native life. Directly it is safe to do so, the natives will always come and live on the beach. They much prefer to do this for every reason, and do not mind walking a long distance every day to their gardens. There is no doubt, I think, that a village where there is a school is more safe from raiders than those which are altogether heathen; therefore all are in favour of schools being erected by the sea, if they will have them at all. I have mentioned raiders. These disturbers of the public peace are very common in these quarters. Sometimes canoes come over from Maleita and suddenly pounce upon villages who are unprepared, and "wipe them out." This last is a significant phrase, and describes well the ruthless nature of such warfare. But often it has been a chief living only a few miles off who has started in the dead of night and at early dawn surprises the sleeping population, murders every one, takes their skulls for his new canoe or house, and paddles back with as much human flesh as his people can dispose of. Close to Wango, one of our school centres, I was shown a village which had been wiped out only a few years ago. The forty skulls then taken are probably still in existence, but the people near a school do not care to talk of such exploits, nor to exhibit their spoils.

In quite early days the first Bishop Selwyn landed on Cristoval, and took some boys to New Zealand. Doubtless Stephen Taroniara may have been one of these. In 1866, Bishop Patteson was at Wango. This village is situated on a beautiful river, in which I had a refreshing bathe early one Sunday morning. Its banks were clothed with sago palms, nutmeg, scarlet hibiscus, areca palms, several varieties of the Pandanus, or screw pine, and the cement tree, as it is called, because from its seeds the natives obtain the substance which makes their canoes watertight. All these were pointed out to me by Mr. Comins. Crocodiles are sometimes seen here, but when they come they are hunted till they die or depart. Above all, Wango is the home of old Takdi. Of him I shall have something to say presently. But to return to Bishop Patteson. He mentions that there were then one hundred houses, but not more than two hundred people. Since then the numbers have still further decreased. The bishop also notices the scarcity of children. Except in the few school villages, indeed, this is one of the sad facts that impresses itself strongly upon any one at the present day. Infanticide is terribly common, almost universal, and it is the old women who are in fault. They are eager to kill babies as soon as they are born, that the young mothers may not be kept from work in the fields, which then would fall heavily upon the old and childless. I asked, of course, in what way the population of a village was kept up. I was told that in all coast villages it is the custom to buy boys and girls of six or eight from the bush people, who apparently do not practise infanticide. When I landed at Wango with a member of the Mission who had not visited it for many years, it was pleasant to hear him exclaim at once, "How delightful it is to see the young children running about! it is a sight we never saw in old days." This result is, of course, the effect of the "new teaching." At the same time, till the present generation of old women passes away, the evil will lurk even in Christian villages. In two places where I landed I was told that in one case two-thirds, in the other one-half, of those I saw had been born in the bush, and had been bought. At the present day the children are not very shy of a white man ; but Bishop Patteson says that in 1866 it took some days before the little one could be persuaded to come near any one who indulged in the strange and abnormal habit of covering his body with cloth.

The firstfruits of Cristoval may be said to have been Stephen Taroniara, who, with a lad named Sumarua, came away with Bishop Patteson, and was taught both in New Zealand and at Norfolk Island. Sumarua I met at Heuru, in this island. Stephen came from Tawatana, which has been already mentioned. He was baptized on July 19, 1868, confirmed on January 24, 1869, and received his first communion on March 28, 1869. During 1868 he was one of the sufferers in the epidemic of typhoid fever at Norfolk Island. He was very ill, and recovered slowly ; and, as was natural, the time of his convalescence was fruitful for his spiritual life, surrounded as he was by the society at the centre of the Mission. It was shortly before he recovered that he said to the bishop, "Everything seems new. You say what you have said before, but it seems now to have new power. I don't think I could ever even wish to think the old thoughts and to lead the old life. What is it ?" "I think you know what it is," said the bishop ; "what power alone can change the thoughts and wishes of the heart?" "I think," he answered slowly, "it must be the work of the Holy Spirit. I feel sure it is, and I thank God for it." It was Stephen who formed one of the crew that rowed the bishop ashore at Nukapu on that fatal day, September 20, 1871. He was struck by many arrows, and when he returned to the ship he knew his end had come. He just said, as he was helped on board, "The bishop and I."

At the present time there are fourteen teachers at work in Cristoval, and three more are being trained at Norfolk Island. The teachers' wives are in some cases doing a quiet and a noble work by the moral influence they exert. At Wango, two women, wives of the two teachers, have been instrumental in saving many a baby's life at the time of his birth. Instructions have been given them to offer their services on such occasions, and to protect the little babe whom the mother desires to save, were she a free agent.

Of course here, as elsewhere, there is a great variety of scholars under instruction. Here are the young who, it is hoped, will learn to read and write; there are the middle-aged and also the grey-headed. One man was pointed out to me as a great warrior; a fine specimen of humanity he certainly was. He would never learn to read, but he had made such good progress in the best of all knowledge that he had been baptized. I asked a few questions when I was there. "Where is Jesus Christ?" "He is in heaven." "Where else is He?" "He is in our hearts." "What did He come on earth to do?" "He came to die, that we might live." "What was His last command?" "He told us to tell all others about Himself." The answers were given without hesitation, and this was the result of the work of a native teacher.

Those who can read at the present time number one hundred and fourteen. There are sixty who are baptized, and the total of all who are listeners is two hundred and thirty.

No account of Cristoval would be complete without some mention of old Takdi, the chief. He is not yet a Christian: and it is likely he never will be, though he has become a different man. He is a firm friend of the Mission. Years ago, when he made his first appearance on the *Southern Cross*, his full dress consisted simply of a waistcoat! Of the old man's past history it is expedient not to say too much. He has been a great warrior, and is a man of decided character, one of the three chiefs I met in my tour who were a real power; and he has had, perhaps, more than his share in those raids of which I have spoken. On the Sunday evening when I said farewell to him he presented me with an old food-bowl, which I value; but it would be as well not to ask too particularly what sort of food it may have held in old days. In 1890 Takdi bought a new canoe; I saw it in all its glory of inlaid pearl-shell, but, alas! the white ants had found their way to it. The canoe is fully thirty feet long, and capable of accommodating a great many people. When he had made it his own the chief was in distress. He had always sacrificed a life on these occasions. Could he forego the usual custom in his old age? His people took the matter into their own hands, and told him that they would, according to the usual practice, take the canoe from village to village, exhibiting it and receiving presents everywhere, but it must be on condition that no life was to be taken. Takdi consented, though it was with gloomy forebodings that his venture would end disastrously. The party started, and were everywhere well received. Even the elements joined in a message of peace, for never were the winds so propitious as they were during this cruise. The presents also were as numerous as ever; but in one respect, however, there was a difference. The villagers in San Cristoval heard that the crew of Takdi's state barge had a chaplain, and went to prayers night and morning to praise and worship the one God.

Slowly infanticide, cannibalism, and many evil customs are receding. But at present nineteen-twentieths of this island is untouched by the Mission. The people are as sheep that have no shepherd. The English staff of the Mission must be increased. Everything must be increased. Our prayers must be more fervent, our help more liberal: then the blessings will follow. The following account of Takdi's son will be read with interest. Takdi had an only son, who he was anxious should be trained at Norfolk Island. He had good abilities, and at length he was baptized Robert Jackson. He could read and write well, and played the harmonium, and was a good draftsman. He was also engaged to Rosa, the only daughter of Stephen Taroniara, who was killed at Nukapu. Rosa had been trained at Norfolk Island also, and the couple were attached to each other; but Robert's Wango friends complained that in consequence of her mission training Rosa did not know how to cook and work like ordinary Wango women, and declared she was no fit wife for their future chief. (I may add here that girls are taught to cook and wash, and mend and make clothes, and to be generally useful at Norfolk Island; but they are not taught to work in the fields. This is where the fault, in their eyes, probably lay.) According to native custom the wife had to be bought for him; but Takdi refused to complete the purchase, and the marriage never took place. Rosa went to relations at Heuru, and married a heathen and died. Robert had to content himself with a heathen wife from the bush, with whom he did not agree. Heathen influences were very strong round him, and his father was most anxious that he should distinguish himself as a warrior. Various expeditions were prepared against neighbouring villages in which Robert had to take part, and the man deteriorated fast in character. He gave up prayers and school, and was fast becoming the savage his father wished him to be. When Mr. Comins came to the district, in 1880, he found Robert living this heathen life, yet ready at the same time to acknowledge how unhappy he was, and his desire to repent. His heathen wife died, or ran away at this time. Soon afterwards he married Suboara, a chief's daughter. She was not baptized, but was in the first class in the school, and an excellent girl. From this time Robert began to amend. After an interval sufficient to test his repentance, he was admitted to school again, but was not allowed to teach. For more than a year he showed the signs of a converted man, and it is said of him that he used to look round the school, note the absentees, and go to them afterwards. In 1882 he was bitten by a shark, and died of the effects. Those who were with him say that he spoke touchingly of his trust in God and his Saviour in his last moments.

One more story of Wango life. It is the history of the life of the first school-teacher there. Michael Bauro was one of Bishop Patteson's boys at Norfolk Island, and the first teacher of the Wango school. He was not a man of high attainments, but a good and an earnest one. His health was bad, but though often laid aside, he struggled on, and kept the school open, in spite of the strong influences of evil in the village, where Takdi lived, all powerful then for evil. On one occasion, when a great many people had assembled at Wango who were mutual enemies, it was Michael who rushed in and prevented the combatants from shedding blood. In 1883 the captain of a labour vessel complained to the bishop that the teacher had come aboard and accused them of immoral practices. It is not certain whether in this case the charge was well founded, but we cannot help rejoicing that a native teacher, left to himself, had the courage to face Englishmen, who too often bear a bad reputation, and are only too ready to resent interference with their pursuits. Michael had a child, to whom he was devoted. Like too many fond parents, he indulged the child till he was in danger of ruining his character; but when his error was pointed out to him, he set himself to rule his child wisely, but in a manner which met with no sympathy among his relatives. The result was, however, that the spoilt child grew up into a well-behaved and steady lad. The teacher's patient work in the school at last began to bear fruit. Many of his people were baptized, and this step is never taken without careful inquiry. The majority of the people, also, of Wango gave up their heathen practices, and came to school. But Michael's illness continued to increase, and it was evident that he was dying of consumption. He knew that his days were numbered. His great anxiety now was to assist Mr. Comins with translations of the Gospels, in order that his people might have the Word of God in their own dialect after he was gone. Often when he was almost too ill to think or speak, he struggled on with his work. On Christmas Day, 1889, he received the Holy Communion for the last time, and in the early days of the New Year he passed peacefully away, a faithful soldier of his Master. These simple stories of the results of Christian teaching in these islands speak for themselves. Let those who value the blessings and means of grace in their own country stretch out their hands to give to these islanders what they themselves have freely received.

I visited two schools in Cristoval besides Wango, one at Haani and another at Heuru. At the last place I met with some of the wildest people I had yet come across. As we walked for about a mile along the shore, I had on one side of me the Rev. R. Comins, and on the other a discontented-looking native, unmistakably a heathen, and swinging a long knife with a blade of about eighteen inches. Upon inquiring who this gentleman was, I was informed that he was the "rain-maker" of the place, and hated the school and all belonging to it. As I looked at him out of the corner of my eye, I bethought myself how much he would have liked to have dropped that knife neatly upon the head of a bishop, and thus try to end the school work. He behaved himself, however, extremely well; and the visit to his village was deeply interesting. The teacher I discovered to be, among other things, the best bowler the Mission had ever had. He had on one occasion disposed of an eleven from a man-of-war for less than twenty runs. The spears and all sorts of curiosities were particularly numerous here, and from one man I bought an orange cowrie for a few sticks of tobacco. These rare shells are often procured at this corner of Cristoval. Last, not least, the Mission had driven a wedge into a degraded district. Some of the faces at Heuru exhibited signs of Christian feeling, but a larger number exhibited every sign of savagery in demeanour and extreme scantiness of clothing. Cristoval still waits to be conquered by the Church.

CHAPTER XVI.

MELEITA (SOLOMON ISLANDS).

THREE schools; seventy-eight baptized one hundred and twenty scholars; two hundred and forty listeners; population unknown.

Two large islands, each about a hundred miles long, form a long reach of sea nowhere very broad. As the ship speeds before the sea breeze going westward, it seems but some ten miles at most from land to land, often less. And what a prospect it is! So full of romance, and so beautiful to the eye. On the left, Guadalcanar reveals a noble range of hills, rising at length to a height of eight thousand feet. They are forest-clad, except at the very peaks. Valleys lead up to them, and shoreward there is an extensive plain, covered with cocoanuts and the usual brilliant foliage. Of this island we must speak in due time. Turn to the right hand, and Maleita, unknown as yet, dark with records of savagery and cannibalism, stretches as far as the eye can see backwards and forwards. The hills are not so lofty, but as I leant over the bulwarks of the

Southern Cross they fascinated me. I could discern columns of smoke rising here and there in the recesses of the valleys. I pictured the rivers running down from the "folded hills," and thought how cool the air must feel far up there above the heated plains by the shore. No white man had ever penetrated these recesses: that was the wonderful thought. Even the Mission ship could not send its occupants with safety into that bush. The natives are, for the most part, entirely unclothed. A fine race physically, and good workers, the Maleita boys are great favourites on the Queensland plantations; but their homes are unvisited by the white men. Labour vessels will send their boats for a certain distance up the rivers, but they will never land their men; and the Church of Christ is certainly not in possession in Maleita, though the next island (Florida), once as wild, is now almost entirely Christian. As I have said before, it is the large islands which at present have presented the most stubborn resistance, but it is certainly not for want of prayerful effort. As early as 1857, the elder Selwyn landed on Maleita, taking with him some Guadalcanar boys. The bishop said he was met by about a hundred men, who were quite friendly, a sure sign that they had not been tampered with by the kidnapper or drunken trader. On his next voyage the bishop touched at Oroha on the south coast, and the chief came away with him, in spite of the strong opposition of his people. I can only account for his action by the extraordinary fascination exercised by that wonderful man over natives of the most savage kind. There are some men whom dogs will never bite; apparently it is the same in regard to the wild Melanesian. I have seen some of them on Maleita who seemed not only savage, but wild; and I can appreciate the cool courage of those frequent and solitary landings in old days as no one can who has not visited these shores. Ignorant of the language, understanding nothing of their special customs, perhaps unacquainted with their special "tapu mark," it required a mixture of coolness and watchfulness which, now that I understand it, elicits one's warmest admiration. But to return to the chief of Oroha. Unluckily, the poor fellow did not preserve his health. He became temporarily insane on board, and had to be tied down during part of the time. And this became a cause of serious trouble when he was brought back to his people, for it is a very grave offence to bind a chief. Visits from the Mission clergy were continued. In 1878 Selwyn the younger was welcomed by the name of Bishooka : an amusing compound of two words of dignity, Bishop and Fishhook, the former prized by the white man, the latter the dream of his black brother. It is by bribery conducted by fishhooks that many great things have, at least, been begun. A story is told, indeed, by the elder Selwyn, I think, that on one occasion, in Mallicolo in the Hebrides, the captain of some vessel landed, and found himself in danger. He kept on repeating "Fishhook!" "Fishhook!" They understood him to mean "Bishop, Bishop," and, concluding the white man belonged to one whom they could trust, they let him go uninjured. The mission has but three schools as yet on this island of one hundred miles, and they are all close together at the southeast end. The oldest is Saa, and it was commenced by the Rev. Joseph Atkin, and he was followed by the Rev. John Still about 1878. Mr. Still rowed with Bishop Selwyn in the Cambridge eight, and in due time he followed his friend to these regions in the cause of duty. The natives were struck by his proportions, and on one occasion he was the recipient of a compliment truly Melanesian. One day a native advanced up to him courteously and silently, holding a straw in his hand. This he ventured delicately to place on Still's nose, then he carefully placed his finger on the straw just at the place where the nose ended. Carefully removing the straw from its resting-place of a moment ago, he broke it off where his finger had been. And what did it all mean? Was it an incantation, a spell, a charm? Nothing of the kind; our friend had been immensely struck by the wonderful nose of this wonderful Englishman, and he simply wished to have a record of the exact length of that feature of his clergyman's face. He took a string and hung that bit of straw up in his house, and brought it out to show to his admiring friends when he wished to astonish them by the sights he had seen. This incident reminds me of a story I heard on board the ship—how that there is a fat man at Norfolk Island, very fat indeed. The Melanesians were permitted to measure the calf of this man's leg and also his waist. In due time the story grew in the islands. The string that measured the stomach was exhibited as that which recorded the size of the calf; and as to the stomach, they declared there was no string on the island that could girth it!

Talking one day with the Rev. C. Bice, he told me of an adventure he had not long ago in Maleita. They knew of a boy who had once been to Norfolk Island, and that he lived up a river not far from Port Adam. The ship took them a certain distance, and then they embarked in their boat and pulled away until the ship was left a long way behind. At length they met a number of canoes full of men entirely unclothed and all armed. They kept on repeating the boy's name, but did not know a word of the language. But the more they repeated the name the more angry the men became. They had also left their boat, and were on shore, and so threatening did matters become that Bice turned to Mr. Forrest, who was with him, and said that he thought their time had come. At length, and not a moment too soon, the very man they were looking for appeared. He came to their rescue, and kept the men back, and informed them that these were friends of his. And he told the Englishmen that the natives supposed they had come to forcibly seize their chief. He urged them to get into their boat at once and row away without him. It would be death to the whole party were he to accompany them. But if the next morning they sent a boat ashore at a certain spot he would be there awaiting them. The next morning, true to his word, the man was where he said he should be. He had walked all night in peril of his life in order to rejoin his old friends.

One morning, at six o'clock, I landed with Mr. Palmer at Saa, and walked up to the village with the camera. It was early, and we had to wait a while for the usual morning service, in which we all joined. The teacher here is a well-known man. Joseph Wate was on board the *Southern Cross* when Patteson was killed at Nukapu, and has always borne a good character. His wife has a charming face, and looked a worthy helpmeet. I took a good photograph of the family, including a crippled boy, who was tenderly nursed by them. Certainly it was easy to see that we were in a wild region. Men entirely unclothed stalked about round us, and others held bundles of spears, which they were ready enough to part with for sticks of the precious tobacco. News came in 1893 that the surrounding natives have made an attack on Joseph Wate's school. They came armed with rifles bought from traders; they killed one of our people and wounded another. Scouts were sent out every morning by Mr. Comins, who was, fortunately, on the spot; but the entire armament of the school people consisted of but three old guns. What the future now may bring forth no man can say; but it is an illustration of the dangers constantly met with. If it is asked what reason there can be for such attacks, the answer probably is that the heathen community may have been informed by some "rainmaker" that the new teaching is a spell of evil omen, and that to wipe out the Christians is the only remedy. In 1892, when the *Southern Cross* arrived at Port Adam in April, the clergy found the school in this place surrounded in the same manner. The ship then took all the school people away, and landed them at Saa, which is about ten miles away. The attacking force thought the Mission ship was a man-of-war, and retired altogether, so it was afterwards discovered, and the school returned to its home in a fortnight. On this occasion it is Saa's turn to be in danger. Let us pass on now to Port Adam. It is a natural harbour formed by a reef and a sort of island; and here a noble fellow named Johnson is the teacher. He is a true missionary, a stranger to Maleita, but one who has devoted himself to God's work, and is ready to go where he may be sent. In 1891 he was nursing a friend of his at Norfolk Island; the lad was ill, and before his death he became unconscious, but in his words he betrayed the spirit that had grown up within him. The words of the Prayer-book were upon his lips; and he repeated over and over again in his delirium the verses of the sixty-seventh psalm, which he had so often sung at evening prayer in the chapel, especially the second verse, "That Thy way may be known upon earth, Thy saving health among all nations." When his spirit passed away, Johnson knelt by the body and dedicated himself to the work for life in the spirit of the words which were ringing in his ears. This was the man I found at his post of danger. He had chosen a wife for himself from among the Port Adam people, and we carried the girl away to Norfolk Island, a true Maleita girl, with a wonderful bone ornament stuck through the cartilage of the nose, and projecting on both sides of her face several inches. No one on board could talk her language except a companion, no older than herself, from the same place. We experienced one of the hottest days of our tour when we were at Port Adam, and even the taking of photographs was an effort; and in the schoolhouse I witnessed a wedding conducted by a clergyman in shirt and trousers and with bare feet. We had brought no canonicals ashore, but doubtless the simple dress of the officiating minister was strictly in accord with their notions, and, judging from what I saw here, a man with shirt and trousers was an exceedingly overdressed person. I did my best to buy from one man his only article of clothing, which consisted of a mother-of-pearl ornament like a large crescent moon, worn round the neck. But neither here nor elsewhere could I tempt any one to part with an ornament of this particular shape. The Maleita men, as a rule, are fine, powerful fellows, extremely well-developed. They are great cannibals also. And at Saa I noticed some who were of a much more pronounced Malay type than any I met elsewhere, with finely cut features and a delicate nose. How this comes about I cannot say. But in these islands the traveller expects to see much that is mysterious connected with the mingling of races—Polynesians, Melanesians, the Malay type, dark men, fair men, some definitely negritic, others betraying a higher type of countenance.

No account of Port Adam in Maleita would be complete without the story of the fate of two Cruzians who were blown away from the Duff group and landed at Port Adam, about one hundred and sixty miles from their home. In 1877 Bishop Selwyn arrived at Port Adam, and discovered that these unfortunates had only reached land to fall into the hands of men who proposed to fatten them and then to eat them. The chief at Port Adam came on board, and from him they learnt the details of their scheme. Then Selwyn offered him "trade" of all kinds, and to an enormous extent, to induce the men to sell him their captives. For a long while it was of no avail, for they had determined to eat them. But, at length, the bribe proved too great a temptation, and one of the Cruzians was saved; he was the thinnest, and was covered with sores; but the bishop sailed away, glad to have saved one life, but feeling that the other captive would be sacrificed. The natives, indeed, seem to have repented of their transaction almost immediately, for that evening the *Southern Cross* was in danger. Canoes were to be seen stealing ahead to dispute the passage out of the harbour, and men were seen cutting down trees or bamboos in order to make rafts to facilitate their attempt to board the ship. Had they succeeded in their object, of course the whole Mission party and crew would have been wiped out. But Captain Bongard is the wariest of men, and no sooner did he notice signs of hostility than he took his ship safely out, and the bishop proceeded on his visitation of the Solomon group. A few weeks later, though it was a dangerous thing to have done, the *Southern Cross* once more entered Port Adam to learn what had taken place. They found the remaining captive still alive, but carefully guarded somewhere in the bush. The chief once more came on board and beheld the man he had been induced to part with, now getting fat, and recovered from his sores. The sight, it is said, made his mouth water, and he gave the ransomed man an affectionate and pressing invitation to come ashore for a while and visit his friend. In vain, however, was the net spread on this occasion, and the man who had once been saved from these cannibals had no intention of setting foot on shore here again. This second visit from the chief at Port Adam must have been an anxious time for the captain of the *Southern Cross*, after the former experiences. Always on such occasions his post is at the gangway, watching the canoes as they come alongside, and taking care that no iron tomahawks come on board. All further negotiations for the release of the remaining captive failed, and the ship sailed away, compelled to leave the man to his fate. But the thrilling part of the story is yet to be related. The captive escaped, after all. On the night preceding the feast this man was sleeping in a house guarded by his captors, awaiting a certain death when the sun rose. But on that night a deep sleep fell upon the Maleita men, and they, who, like all natives, sleep as lightly as wild beasts as a general rule, never awoke when their victim raised himself stealthily up and then proceeded to make his way to the door and then to the shore. Here he discovered a canoe, but there was no paddle in it. Accordingly, he retraced his steps, entered the hut once more, passed his guards, took a paddle from the thatch of the roof, and for the third time made his escape past them. Then, entering the canoe, he paddled away until he had put some miles between himself and Port Adam, when he broke up the canoe and the paddle, and hid the pieces and took to the bush. After a week he discovered Saa, and was just about to step into the open there when he suddenly observed the Port Adam chief and his men questioning the natives. He fled once more, but after another week he began to despair of his position, stranded in a hostile island far from his home, and he determined to surrender himself to the Saa people and meet his fate, whatever it might be. Fortunately for him the chief of Saa took a fancy to him, and adopted him, and here he was discovered by the bishop on his next trip, was ransomed, and returned to his home in Nufilole, on Reef Island. This man used to declare that it was the bishop's God that sent his captors to sleep. One of these men went to Norfolk Island, but whether either of them ever were baptized I cannot say. The names of the men who had so wonderful an escape were Tefonu and Akua. But the immediate effect of their deliverance by the Mission ship was evident. These men knew Natei of Nelua, in Santa Cruz, about whom I have already written so much. Now, at length, what Patteson yearned to do, and failed to accomplish, was about to come to pass. A footing was to be obtained on this difficult island. The rescued men recommended the bishop and his people to Natei as good and kind men who meant them no harm, and the days of fruitless rowing along the shores of Santa Cruz were numbered. The door was opened, and the conquest of Santa Cruz was begun. There is something, indeed, dramatic in the whole incident, and God opened through a deed of kindness in another place a way for the Mission which could not by direct means be commenced at all. It is a parable, indeed, of much of our experience in this world in the prosecution of many undertakings. I have tried to depict these natives in their own homes, though it is not easy to give an adequate realization of a Maleita man with his ornaments. Their clubs are hard to obtain now; most symmetrical objects they are, especially when covered with fine matting, red and yellow in colour. The same wicker-work is used for their combs and armlets; and at Alite, on their coast, there is a regular establishment for the grinding and preparation of native shell money. I believe it is a large industry, and supplies all the neighbouring islands. The spears, too, are handsome; but what can be said of their nose ornaments! The long bone ornament worn transversely across their faces has already been mentioned. In addition to this, some of them will pierce as many as eighteen holes in a circle round the nostrils, and plug them all neatly with pieces of mother-of-pearl, giving the appearance of a ring set with stones. If in addition to this they insert in a hole at the very tip of the nose a shell ornament ending in the head of a tropic bird, and projecting straight out from the face, you have some idea of the elegant appearance of a Maleita beau, who may possibly consider any other articles of dress absolutely unnecessary.

Let us now shift the scene from Maleita to Fiji. There are hundreds of Maleita boys working on the Fiji sugar plantations; and though work among the Fijians themselves is left to the Wesleyans, still here among the Solomon Islanders the Church of England is only following up her own people.

The Rev. Mr. Jones, of Suva, and the Rev. Mr. Floyd, of Levuka, are both deeply interested in the work. I spent only one afternoon at Levuka, where Mr. Floyd has been stationed for many years, but I heard of the fifty Solomon Islanders who attended his ministrations. But at Suva I had a better opportunity. On my first evening in Mr. Jones's house, as I was sitting in the drawing-room, some quiet, well-behaved Melanesians came in, knelt down before me, kissed my hand and sat down on the floor. Upon inquiring who they were I was informed that they were Maleita boys; and in talking to them I discovered that they had become Christians through the good work done in Suva by Mr. Jones and his wife and other workers. A good many of them expressed their readiness to go back to their own country, wherever we might choose to send them, in order to teach their people what they had learnt themselves. I confess that the experiences of that evening opened up to me quite a new field of thought. I had visited Maleita. I had realized that, except where our three schools exist, the whole island was still given over to savagery and cannibalism. No white man's life was safe on those shores. And here, in Fiji, what a change was visible! Men clothed and in their right mind—men who had been brought away by the reviled labour-traffic system. Yet out of the old and most evil practices there had emerged much that was very good where these opportunities had been utilized. The labour ships are now well managed, and kidnapping, at least in English ships, is a thing of the past. The plantations had effected for these people what the Mission upon the spot has at present failed to do, at least to any great extent. Of course, there are immense advantages for mission work to Fiji. Just as boys and girls brought to Norfolk can be trained best away from their homes, so on a plantation where godliness reigns there are unquestionably great advantages for Christian work. I was more and more interested as the hours passed at Suva, to learn about the hundred and fifty Melanesians attending their school night after night, of the earnest-minded ladies who assisted, and of the communicants among these Maleita men. Before I left I confirmed eighty-three of them; many had been communicants for years waiting anxiously for a bishop's visit, delayed at this time for six years. And, in conversation with one of the lady workers, I heard that some of these men lived together in well furnished little houses, and that one only a few days before had given four pounds ten shillings for a kerosene lamp to brighten his home. My visit, all too short to this lovely place, was terminating; and as I walked on to the quay I was met by some native gentlemen, who came politely forward to wish me farewell. I discovered that these were my Confirmation candidates of a few hours before. These were natives of an island where life can hardly be an ideal existence. It was then borne in upon me with force that the labour traffic could be made a mighty engine for the conversion of the South Seas, and that what was once a curse might prove a blessing in Christian hands. I am convinced that you cannot isolate the South Sea Islands. It is better to regulate intercommunication and to utilize the openings as they are being utilized in Fiji. But the work there is great, and we should have a clergyman engaged altogether in this work at Suva. Most thankful am I to know that my visit to Suva was followed by one from Dr. Codrington, the honoured veteran of the Melanesian Mission, and I have read with joy how much struck he was at the possibilities of the openings here. Maleita, indeed, may yet be quickly won by the help of work in the plantations. Nor is the direct effort of this Mission at a stand. We hope to hear every day that Dr. Welchman has established himself at the north end of Maleita, going over from his own island to Ysabel.

In concluding this account of Maleita, I must not omit to mention what the captain of a labour vessel told me he had seen in one of the harbours on the Maleita coast. His vessel was anchored inside a reef in still and deep water. The natives came to him and asked him to keep his ship perfectly still, and to avoid all splashing. They then drove before them, with shouts and yells, a large shoal of porpoises—numbering, I think, one hundred and twenty—until they all stranded themselves on a shelving beach; they were then despatched with spears and clubs. It must have been a grand harvest for these men, since porpoise teeth are a recognized currency in these islands.

CHAPTER XVII.

GUADALCANAR (SOLOMON ISLANDS).

NO schools; population unknown.
It is as well that the Christian worker has sometimes to put his hand upon his mouth and confess failure. Perhaps if all missionary reports were always open in giving their experience the failures would be more frequently alluded to. Indeed the wonder is that success is so quickly attained, considering the imperfect instruments engaged in the work (fallible men of like passions with ourselves), considering also the grudging support given by the Church at large. Above all it is not wonderful if progress is delayed, for the task is nothing less than to change the very springs of action to introduce a new power into the life, and to change every thought and aspiration of the heart. To God be praise Who so quickly gives to our efforts in His name more than we ask or think. Guadalcanar is the great failure of the Melanesian Mission so far as outward signs are any test, but it is for no lack of attempts. There is something mysterious about it indeed, for it can hardly be called so

difficult an island as Malcita or even as Cristoval. But the fact has to be stated plainly, and with sorrow, that there are no Christian stations or schools in Guadalcanar. It is all the more distressing when we remember that there must be dozens of Guadalcanar men in the plantations in Queensland and Fiji, who, by the exertions of Christian people, have been truly converted. The question cannot fail to press for an answer, what becomes of them when they return home? Do they relapse into barbarism because they are as sheep scattered over the mountains, shepherdless? At gatherings for prayer, at missionary meetings, there can hardly be a more forcible argument for renewed exertion upon the part of all than the fact that good work done among the plantations is being to all appearance lost by the lack of success, at present, of the Mission in the island home itself. It would be indeed a turning of the tables upon us if the reproach came not from the Church to the labour traffic, but from the labour traffic to the Church in this instance. The fact remains, as I have stated, that wilder islands have been attacked with success. Lands beyond Guadalcanar have been almost entirely won; but this great tract, so fair to behold, so striking to the eye, with its lofty range of mountains culminating in the huge bulk of Mount Lammas eight thousand feet high, remains obstinately heathen. It is a good discipline, and it is certainly a call to duty. Guadalcanar is, of course, more or less an unknown territory—I suppose very little of its extent; one hundred miles in length by some thirty in breadth, is familiar to Europeans. Naturalists, like Mr. Woodford, have lived on its shores, but have found it impossible to proceed more than a few miles inland. The natives of one village dare not travel far; and languages quickly change. I doubt whether any one, native or English, has ever approached the highest peak, much less climbed it. Yet the *Southern Cross* sails past its shores twice a year at least. Dozens of times has the Mission tried to succeed, but without permanent success. People in the neighbouring islands tell stories of the wild men of Guadalcanar. "In Florida," says Dr. Codrington, "they believe that on the mountains of Landari—the part of Guadalcanar near their own island—there are wild men whom they call Mumoulu. They are men, and have a language, the hair of their heads is straight and reaching down their legs; their bodies are covered with long hair, and they have long nails; they are large and tall, but not above the size of men. One was killed not long ago, the coast people of Landari say, and so they know very well what they are like. They live in caves in the mountains, they plant nothing and eat snakes and lizards, and they eat any coast man they can catch. They carry on their backs bags filled with pieces of obsidian with which to pelt men whom they see, and they set nets round trees to catch men who have climbed them; they use spears also." Such an extract reveals to us how little is really known yet of these regions.

Let me now make it clear to my readers that the Mission has worked hard to get a footing in Guadalcanar. The first Bishop Selwyn landed in 1857 at Marau Sound at the south-eastern extremity. It is a capital anchorage, land-locked, and extending among numerous islands. It was not by any means the first visit, for on this occasion scholars, who had spent a season in New Zealand, were returned to their homes. At the next visit in the ensuing year, we are told that great friendliness was shown. Crowds wanted to go back with the bishop to his strange and wonderful home far away. So anxious were they about it that they began quarrelling among themselves for the privilege, until they were quietly informed by the bishop that the choice rested with him alone. It is obvious, indeed, that this was the only course, for it would be useless to bring away old men and confirmed heathens in place of members of the younger generation upon whose active influence for good the Mission might hereafter rely. We are also informed that at this time the natives were arrant thieves. In 1859 these people again crowded the ship's deck, and could hardly be persuaded to go ashore. "Twenty-six slept on board, thirteen in the bishop's cabin." I wonder whether my readers can realize the significance of the extract. Do they know the peculiar odour of black flesh? Do they appreciate the strong stomach of the first bishop as well as his brave heart, when in the tropics the little cabin of a twenty-five-ton schooner contained thirteen black men besides the white bishop? This is, however, a mere detail. In the morning, the account goes on to tell us, sixty canoes came alongside, and nine lads remained. But eight years afterwards it is related by Bishop Patteson that the Guadalcanar lads were most unsatisfactory. They wished to leave Norfolk Island as soon as ever the novelty had worn off. No effect was produced upon them by the atmosphere of peace and regular labour by the example of the high-minded bishop and his staff. While all other scholars felt these influences, they did not; and the trouble taken with them seemed practically to be wasted, at least in comparison with efforts made elsewhere. The bishop therefore decided that unless these natives were more in earnest he could not afford to take away any more. The visits gradually ceased, and though Florida, close by, is virtually Christian, Guadalcanar throughout its great length and breadth contains no Christian station. One interesting detail I extract as to the novel way of feeding pigs here. A woman was watched as she took cocoanuts and threw them with all her force at one of the big hollowed-out trees which form the native drums. The noise made attracted the pigs, who fed at the same time upon the repast prepared by way of dessert in this manner.

In 1883 the Rev. W. Ruddock spent three months at the north-western end of Guadalcanar. He called first at a place where two young fellows who were with him were born, hoping to get an opening thus. But there were hostilities between the different villages at the time. So they proceeded to Vaturanga to a chief who had permitted two boys to go to Norfolk Island in 1881. He was friendly, and willing that a school should be started; but he and his thirty wives lived in a village by themselves, and he insisted that the school should be near his house and away from all other people. There is a humorous side to this picture certainly, as we imagine this potentate adding to his harem a school for the purpose of self-aggrandisement, evidently for no other purpose. Little indeed could be effected, and when a chief came over from Savo, a neighbouring island, this man, Kouna by name, persuaded his friend to have nothing more to do with the new teaching. No more boys were permitted to go to Norfolk Island, and the attempt failed. But it is interesting to trace the career of one of the two boys who accompanied Mr. Ruddock. Hugo Gorovaka is his name. I met him in 1892 at Bugotu, in Ysabel, where he was head teacher at Soga's village, and a man of character and decision. He returned with us to Norfolk Island, and has since been ordained. It is certain therefore that he will come back to his own people in Guadalcanar and attempt to give them "the new teaching." At the present moment also there is a lad at Norfolk Island from Guadalcanar named Barnabas Vahea, of Ruavatu. But the feeling against the step he has taken is so strong among his own people that when he left Norfolk Island for a holiday he was unable to return to his home, but went to some relations in Florida. I have mentioned these cases of individual converts in order to show that Guadalcanar has its real converts in the Mission, but as yet no regular centre of work; and it may soon have its native clergyman.

I am proud to say that I had the honour of landing on Guadalcanar, and as it is the only instance which was presented to me of an unwelcome visit from the Mission I proceed to narrate it. As we sailed along between Guadalcanar and Maleita we approached a spot named Aola on the former island. It is a traders' station, nor can there be any doubt that it has exerted a most pernicious influence upon the natives around. A village is situated some three miles from it, and here in April, 1892, a teacher, who had relatives in the place, had been put down in the hope that he might exert an influence over the people. It was September in the same year when we landed, and, of course, nothing had been heard of him since he had been deposited there, five months before. We effected a landing full of hope that at length some definite foothold might have been obtained. It must be confessed, however, that the aspect of affairs was not favourable. As we approached the shore we saw a solitary figure awaiting us; no one else was visible. This looked ominous; and so indeed it was. Alfred, the teacher, said that all his attempts had been entirely frustrated. When he came the chief had said to him, "We shall be glad to see you at any time, for you are one of us; but we do not want the new teaching; we shall have nothing to do with it." Alfred discovered that whenever he opened a book for any purpose (even to read to himself) immediately every one rose up and left the hut; even the children disappeared, and it was clear that strict injunctions had been given to boycott the Christian teaching in this manner. There was nothing for it, he said, but to be taken away. We therefore walked up to the village; no one met us, for every one seemed to be in hiding. The people had gone out of their houses and were watching our movements from among the trees. We passed through an enclosure which, by the way, was adorned with a row of skulls, and found ourselves before the house where Alfred had been living. One by one he brought his goods out, and after waiting to see whether any one would come and greet us, we turned back laden with his few cooking utensils and a box. When we reached the shore one or two people appeared, but they were very shy and distinctly cold. Nothing could have shown this more clearly than the way in which my own advances were received. Before stepping into the boat I offered sticks of tobacco to the few who were standing there. But instead of accepting it thankfully and eagerly, there was an evident unwillingness to touch the gift, and very reluctant hands were held out towards me. I remarked upon this to the others, and then Alfred told us that five months before, when Comins had been there and had offered an old man a stick of tobacco, the poor fellow had been afraid to smoke it, as he firmly believed it was administered as a charm by means of which he would become a Christian whether he would or no. The same belief was operating on them when I offered them my peace-offering. We were also told that the reason why the school was so much opposed by the chief consisted in the fact that this village drew a large income from aiding the traders' station not far off in the indulgence of profligacy, and they knew that all such doings would receive a deathblow if the Christian teachers once obtained a footing. A very dark side of the picture is thus unfolded. Savo, the little island mentioned above, is a trader's station. It was the Savo chief who checked Ruddock in his attempt. It was the traders' station at Aola which destroyed the hopes of the efforts at the village which I visited. Mission work has no greater enemy than the ungodly white man, for the foes within the household deal the most deadly blows. The work at Savo itself has indeed long ceased, because of the hostility of "traderized" natives. But though I speak so bitterly of this difficulty, it must be remembered that all traders are not bad or immoral. And how then is Guadalcanar to be won? Will it be by, in this case, departing from the regular plan of the Mission? As every rule has its exception, it may be that in place of beginning with a native scholar trained at Norfolk Island, one of the white clergy will be compelled to locate himself here with perhaps a set of Christian "returned labourers," and thus the open door may be found. Nothing will give greater joy to the staff of the Mission or to those who work and pray for its welfare than to hear that at length one school at least has been established here. We waited long for the open door into Santa Cruz, but it was shown to us at last. Without doubt it will be no different in the case of Guadalcanar.

ULAUA.

Three schools; one hundred and ten baptized; one hundred and twenty attending school; two hundred and forty listeners; population unknown.

Ulaua, or Contrariété, is a small island perhaps ten miles by four, not far from the south-east end of Maleita. Its coral formation is unmistakable, for the distant view of it reveals its terrace-like formation, each one receding from the next below it till the hill in the middle is reached standing about one thousand feet high. The water is very deep on the western or lee side; it was remarkable how close we had to steam before soundings were reached, and it was surprising to me to hear the mate near the bridge sing out thirty fathoms at the same moment that the anchor touched bottom in twenty-one fathoms, so steep was the bottom. In recounting this some months afterwards to a naval officer, he told me what happened there in his own case. They also had anchored here. At night, when his watch began, he went on deck and looked round, and sang up to the quarter-master to ask where the land was! That officer also peered into the darkness and looked confused when no coral shore was visible. The fact is that the ship had drifted away some distance in the darkness, the anchor having been literally hung on to the side of a wall. Of course it would have been impossible to have drifted the other way, and there was no danger drifting westward.

There is a record of a visit to Ulaua by the first

bishop in 1857, in the days when it was a cannibal island. When they were returning to the ship they saw a canoe holding forty men paddling towards them. The Mission party thought that they had come out for a hostile purpose, but as they could not avoid the danger the next best course was boldly to steer straight for the strangers. Apparently the nervousness was mutual, for as soon as the whaleboat approached, the canoe and its occupants bore away as fast as paddles could hurry them. Ulaua is to be a bright spot in the Mission, chiefly owing to the devoted work of the Rev. Clement Marau, who is a true missionary. He is a native of Merelava, in the Banks Islands, and brother of the Rev. William Vaget, whom I ordained in 1892. It is delightful to read of the way in which Clement came to Ulaua. When at Norfolk Island he became godfather to an Ulaua boy called Waaro. This lad in due course went back to Ulaua as one of the first teachers, and Clement wished to do what he could to strengthen his godson's faith, and accordingly accompanied him to start him in his work. It ended in Clement marrying an Ulaua woman, and now he is one of the native priests of the Mission, and one also who has an unstained record for devotion and blameless character. There are now three schools. But Clement has had his great perils to encounter also, for undoubtedly the population was savage and dangerous. One day some natives from the other side of the island came to him and asked if they might pick a cocoanut. He gave them leave, suspecting nothing. In reality they had, according to Ulauan usage, asked him for a man's life, and I do not know how Clement managed to evade the result. Ulauans bury their dead in the sea; the consequence is that the sharks are well accustomed to human flesh, and it is a dangerous bathing-place. The sharks here are looked upon as sacred, and "if a sacred shark—one that had become well known—had attempted to seize a man and he had escaped, the people would be so much afraid of the shark's anger that they would throw the man back again into the sea to be drowned." The usual landing-place for the Mission is one near the principal school, where Clement lives. It is a lovely spot, among great coral boulders, covered with vegetation, and the landing is a sort of scramble up these rocks. A few years ago a poor girl named Amina was brought back from Norfolk Island in an advanced stage of consumption to die among her own people. When this difficult landing-place was reached, the natives set up a shout and said that no woman was permitted to use the spot; they pointed at the same time to a sort of coral cliff some fifteen feet high and more than perpendicular. Up this place the poor girl had to be dragged in spite of her exhausted condition. Amina died soon afterwards. By her side in her last days used to lie her New Testament, and in it were written the names of many for whom she used to pray daily, among them were the names of her four or five godchildren saved, as she herself had been, from heathenism. She never omitted to pray for them. Surely such a life sets us an example and speaks well for the prevailing influence of the Mission in these Southern Seas. It was a Sunday when we landed at Ulaua, and for this reason we took no photographs here according to our custom, though I partly regret it now, especially if a few such pictures might have helped to spread still further the interest in the Mission. I met on that day at the morning service a man named William Wese; he is a man with a naturally bad temper, and years ago, when Bishop Selwyn was distributing presents in one of their houses, William was not satisfied with what he had received. He took up the axe and dashed it with all his force into the ground at the bishop's feet, and no doubt it required strong nerves to be unmoved and show no signs of nervousness. William had been under instruction some time when I saw him, and I was told that not long before, on a certain day, he had felt his temper rising, and made at once for the seashore where he paced up and down for some hours until he could command himself, another instance of the effect of Christian teaching.

Ulaua is famous for its bowls and model canoes and woodwork inlaid with mother-of-pearl. The ship does not buy anything on Sunday; but on Monday morning as soon as it was light the bargaining was very brisk, and bowls and tobacco changed hands to a very large extent. The following facts are worth relating, as giving an insight to the difficulties of Mission work. In 1891 Clement started a school at the north end of the island. Soon afterwards the chief died, and his death was attributed to the school. So strong was the hostility that the teacher had to be withdrawn, and a price was even put upon Clement's head; it is evident, therefore, that even now Ulaua is a post of danger. A remarkable story is also told of Clement's godson, Waaro. There was a strong party who hated his school; but the chief, though he was a heathen, always liked Waaro. At length the chief was lying upon his deathbed, and was deserted by his people. Waaro came to him, and said, "Of course it is our duty to nurse you, and not to desert you as the others have done. But I suppose you would not let us look after you."

"Yes," said the dying man. "Take me into your house and teach me; I have not much longer to live." Waaro took him in; but at the same time he knew what the result would be. The chief would die on Christian ground, and the school people would, of course, be accused of having caused his death. Now many a man would have been tempted to neglect his duty in this predicament. But Waaro did not hesitate. He took the chief home, and taught him and prayed with him till he died. Then at once the cry was raised, "The school has caused our chief's death." The heathen party held a consultation, and then came to Waaro and asked him to come out to them. They were in fact about to kill him, but hesitated to do so in his own house, and the teacher refused to come. "Kill me," he said, "if you like in the schoolhouse; but this is my place. I will not leave it." The question was debated till the evening, and then the tide turned in his favour. They seemed to admire his courage, and they knew, of course, that he had simply taken their chief out of kindness to die in his house. They therefore came back once more, but this time it was simply to ask for the body for burial, and Waaro's life was spared. I trust these simple stories do not tire my readers; it is just in this way that we realize the true romance and pathos of life under difficulties.

No one who has been to Ulaua on a very hot day is likely to forget a little bathing place in a sort of rocky cleft. The stream flows over the face of a rock about eight feet high, and the natives fix bamboos so that the water emerges from four or five of these pipes in so many spouts. It is not unusual when the *Southern Cross* is here to see three or four missionaries in the intervals of their labours sitting side by side under these self-same spouts to their unmixed satisfaction. Even bishops have been detected in the same posture and have survived it. The clergyman in charge of this district was one day enjoying a quiet bathe here when a party of Malanta men from Port Adam, headed by their chief, a noted cannibal, made their appearance. They proceeded to examine the cleric's clothes as they lay on the bank, and even, I believe, essayed to try some of them on. They then turned their attention to the white man himself, and in a most affectionate manner examined his skin and pinched his arms. Whether visions of feasts passed before their eyes I do not know, but the victim told me that he was much relieved when he was once more left to himself. Comins had given them a piece of soap, and told them how to use it, and then slipped away.

Cristoval, Ulaua, Maleita, and, I suppose, Guadalcanar, are at present under the superintendence of one white clergyman. It is not difficult therefore to detect the immense and the immediate need of a larger staff.

Perhaps it will also be of interest if I here insert a simple sentence in seven at least of the dialects known to Mr. Comins.

"Where do you live, and where are you going?"
Wango—Ioe o oa iei mao ari iei?
Fagani—Igo go oga ifei ma go rago ifei?
Saa—Io o oo idei na o ke lae idei?
Manoto—O to ifai na lei fai?
Tawanichia—O io ihei na o lae ihei?
Ulaua—O ioio ihei na oa lae hei?
Ugi—O neneku ihei ma oa lae ihei?

CHAPTER XVIII.

FLORIDA (SOLOMON ISLANDS).

TWENTY-EIGHT schools; three thousand baptized; one thousand and sixty-seven scholars; three thousand five hundred listeners; four thousand population.

If Guadalcanar is at present our great failure, Florida has been our most signal triumph of late years, and those who wish to get a first-rate account of the natives and of God's work among them ought to lose no time in purchasing the Rev. A. Penny's delightful book entitled "Ten Years in Melanesia." It is a fascinating account of his work in Florida, and abounds in details of native life and of personal adventure, which, of course, I cannot hope to furnish in like degree. I spent only three days in Florida, and am simply a gleaner in other men's fields. On an ordinary map, on which Maleita is about half an inch in length, Florida disappears altogether. It is but a speck in comparison, at the western end of the straits between Maleita and Guadalcanar. But what appears to be one little island is in reality a group of three, separated by narrow channels;

and if small islets, in some cases, not an acre in extent are counted, there are more than fifty such islands. Florida is, I think, the loveliest spot in the Solomons. As the ship approaches, the eye is charmed by the sight of open spaces of meadow-like country among the fantastic hills. It is so uncommon an experience that it is hard to believe it. Accustomed everywhere to the depressing appearance of dense, tropical foliage, varied only by brown yam patches, it is refreshing indeed to look upon open pastures. I am told, however, that these so-called meadows are really clothed with a rough grass at least as high as the waist, and often much taller. A lovely reach or strait between two divisions of Florida is called "the Sandfly Channel." But it is another of these strange passages which is most indelibly impressed upon every visitor to Florida. There is a harbour at a spot named Mboli, interesting in itself, inasmuch as in the very middle of it a circular coral reef is springing up some quarter of a mile in diameter, and revealing the contour perfectly. In the deep water passage round it the native fishing stations are erected in great numbers; queer-looking structures, composed of a most insecure perch for a man and several poles between which the net is spread, which is lowered to the bottom and suddenly raised to enclose the fish. Upon the shore close by are visible the native houses and the spacious and really splendid church, a specimen of like structures in many parts of Florida. They are noble pieces of bamboo work, capable of holding three or four hundred people, with a high pitched roof not less than thirty feet in height. They are famous for their singing also in Florida. It is here that you can listen to all the parts taken by large bodies of men

Church at Honggo, Florida.

and women, though it is strange to hear the amen pronounced ameni, and to listen to the late Rev. Mr. Plant called Pulaneti. (Natives here cannot conclude a word with a consonant, or pronounce two consonants together.) Let my reader imagine to himself such a building made of beautifully interlaced bamboo strips and crowned with a massive palm-leaf thatch, with doors cut high, compelling a step of two or three feet—in order that the pigs may not come to church—with no windows, because it is better to get light through the chinks of the wall than heat through windows; imagine this striking edifice planted in the midst of a mass of crotons ablaze with their leaves of crimson and gold and rich shades of every tint, and you have one of the most beautiful effects of tropical scenery, commingled with the associations of happy Christian life in the South Seas. But the greatest object of interest in Mboli harbour is still to be mentioned. A stranger would imagine that the last thing the captain of the *Southern Cross* would do would be to steam suddenly towards the shore circling round the centre reef. But this is what he actually does, turning so sharply at one point, that one can almost shake hands with the people on a point of land; one more corner is turned, and now a narrow channel is visible, previously entirely concealed, the water is evidently deep, and the surface is unruffled. Is it a river, for the current may be setting strongly seaward? No; the water is quite salt. This is in reality one of the mouths of the most extraordinary natural features I have ever seen. It is a deep channel cutting Florida in half from sea to sea, and the tide flows with refreshing force right through it. Straight down the centre of this, and without abating her speed, the *Southern Cross* is steered;

we might be in a river, for the channel is sometimes only one hundred yards broad, though it widens out in places and forms a broad reach at a spot halfway, which has been called Bongard Bight. On both sides the vivid green of the tropical vegetation clothes the banks. Here and there mangroves flourish with their brilliant colouring, and above us there tower hills hundreds of feet high, with their wealth of trees and creepers, and displaying naked cliffs and precipices, standing out proudly from the heights overhead. For sixteen miles at full speed we keep our course, and the fascination of the scene keeps the Mission party on deck. At length the river-like channel opens out into a broad reach, and we have an ocular demonstration that Florida has been cut in two, Gaeta is reached from Mboli. At one point I am told that a reef runs across this saltwater river with seventeen feet of water over it; were this removed the largest vessels could pass through, and as a means of inland navigation it is impossible to overrate its importance. Further west "the Sandfly Channel" separates Mboli from Olevuga. All alike in Mission reports are called Florida. But it is time to turn to the moral and spiritual life of this lovely spot. In 1875, there was no really settled school in Florida. The captain of the ship told me also that in those days no natives were wilder, none more arrant thieves than in Florida; and every door and port-hole had to be closed ere these people were invited on board. And at the present time the Christians are numbered by thousands; in fact, the few heathen are simply waiting to be taught ere they give up their old beliefs.

I have alluded to the splendid churches in Florida; the canoe houses are also works of art. At Mboli, in early days, one was standing which was one hundred and eighty feet long and forty-two feet high. In it was a canoe, fifty-six feet long, six feet beam, and four feet deep. There is much that is intensely interesting in the accounts of those early days. The first clergyman who stayed here was warned by Selwyn not to live in one place, "for," said he, "the chief of the place will become liké the old Maori in New Zealand who boasted of his tame Pakeha." In those days I learn that there was no such thing as a single woman in these islands. If a girl was not married she was the common property of all. Children were named before birth, there being no distinction of sex in the names given. About 1857, the first Selwyn landed here; indeed that wonderful man seemed to have landed everywhere in that year, carrying his life in his hand daily as much as did our noble men and women that same year in India, where the great mutiny had broken out. He met eighty of these wild men on a reef, and one boy came away with him. In 1866 the first clergyman came to reside for awhile. In 1870, he ordered a house to be built for him on a certain spot, whilst he was away at Norfolk Island. The natives jeered at the man who proposed to build it. "You will never see the white man again or his money." Such a house is thus described, twenty feet by ten at the ridge pole; built on piles seven feet high, furnishing a nice cool place to sit, under the flooring; all made of bamboo and palm, with a row of posts, each one higher than the other, forming the steps up which all who wish to enter must jump; and when it has been raining, and the visitor has canvas shoes on, it is a matter of difficulty to keep one's balance on these strange steps. There are no windows, but the light comes through the chinks in the wall; the door is three feet high and eighteen inches wide, and is closed in rain or great heat. I heard a great deal in Florida about the terrible kidnapping days. Indeed, when one hears of the death of a white man now, one asks instinctively what crime the white man or some one before him has committed. In 1872 the crew of the *Lavinia* were murdered here. What else indeed could be expected of these insulted natives? Not long before one hundred Florida men had been deceived and kidnapped; there is even a story that the ship which perpetrated this atrocity was in league with head hunters, and that eighteen of the kidnapped men were handed over to the cannibals. I met an old teacher in Florida who told me that in his youth he had been out in a canoe with some others, and a ship came alongside and threw iron into the canoe and sank it, and took all the men away as labourers, himself among them. It has seemed to me that such terrible deeds must have made Mission work almost impossible. Let it be remembered that the causes of failure in any of these islands so long the centre of unprincipled labour traffic in days gone by, may be attributed to the memories of foul wrong done by our own race to these people.

The man whose name stands out most clearly as a noble Christian is Charles Sapibuana. Just as Mota has George Sarawia, and Vanua Lava has Edwin Wogale, and Motlav Henry Tagalana, and Merelav Clement Marau and William Vaget, and Cristoval Stephen Taroniara, so Florida has her Charles Sapibuana. In 1866 he was brought to New Zealand by Bishop Patteson, being then about twelve. There at Kohimarama, and at St. Barnabas, Norfolk Island, he received the teaching which was to bear such fruit. His course of training was only broken by the usual holiday spent among his own people every two years, and was continued till 1877, when he with his wife and child—for during the last two years at Norfolk Island he had married—settled at Gaeta, his native island, to begin work as a teacher. The ground there was entirely unbroken. If any attempt at a school had been made before this date, they were only such as he and other Gaeta scholars had been able to make during their holidays. He was soon at work, and at once his power began to be felt, for from the first he set himself against what was wrong with quiet and unflinching determination. Of course he met with bitter and dangerous opposition, but he passed unhurt through all, though the threats of vengeance and the plans to kill him might well have daunted a less determined man. The conversion of his brother, and his brother's wife, who were baptized in 1878 was the firstfruit of his labours; from it the rise and progress of Christianity in Florida may be said to date. In 1882 he was ordained deacon in the presence of his people, and from this time till he left Gaeta, at the end of 1885, for Norfolk Island, the increase of his work was even more marked; whilst his influence among all, whether Christian or heathen, proportionately developed. But of late years his health had greatly failed, and he required rest and care. The time also had come when a priest from among his own people was needed to minister to the spiritual wants of the native Church, and surely Charles Sapibuana was one who had used the office of a deacon well. "I advised him therefore," says Mr. Penny, "to return with me to Norfolk Island, hoping that a visit there would restore him to his former strength, and would moreover enable him in the quiet time to prepare for the priesthood.

But it was not to be. When we arrived nearly every one was ill—an epidemic of influenza of a very severe type had taken possession of the island. Sooner or later we all caught it. In Charles's case it developed pleuro-pneumonia, and he passed away on the morning of the Twenty-third Sunday after Trinity." Perhaps my readers would like to see an extract from Charles's note-book. Here is the record of a lesson he had received in 1872: "January 6, Epiphany. This is the great day of the wise men. Jesus was manifested to them, coming from the east to Jerusalem, and seeking the King of the Jews. And to these was Jesus first manifested; and after them to the Romans, and so on until now, when it has reached us. And why was Jesus manifested to the Gentiles? This is why. Only the people of Israel alone knew the way of life, which began with Abraham; and God told Abraham that His people should follow that way. But hitherto we did not know it, and for this cause Jesus came down that He might save us all; and therefore He was manifested to the Gentiles as He was manifested to the Gentiles of old, so is He now to us, in holy washing and the holy food. God helped the Gentiles that they might believe. In like manner we can do nothing of ourselves; but God helps us by manifesting Himself to us." Every one who knew Sapibuana respected him. Had he lived he would have been a great power. "But," as John Wesley said, "God buries His workmen, but carries on His work."

CHAPTER XIX.

FLORIDA (*continued*).

NE of the causes which led to the conversion of Florida was the murder of Lieutenant Bower, of H.M.S. *Sandfly*, in 1880. This little vessel, with a crew of thirty men, was cruising about in these waters when one day Bower took a boat and landed with a few men on a little island named Mandoliana. He and the men were bathing, and anticipated no danger; but on the mainland, about two miles off, a chief named Kalekona permitted a party to paddle across and try and surprise them. Kalekona was in a rage about some stolen money, and was demanding a life instead, hence his action. But there was no cause of complaint whatever against the *Sandfly*. One of the party was Vuria, Kalekona's son, who afterwards gave information, and for this his life was spared. Vuria gives the following account: "We landed on the other side of the point just as the sun was setting, and we crept through the bushes till we could see the sailors on the beach. Three were bathing on the beach, one was cooking, and the captain was standing over

there, drawing in a book. We waited till we thought the right time had come, and then Holambosa gave the sign, and we all rushed out. . . . We fell on the men with our tomahawks. Their guns were in the boat and on the sand; but we were between them and the guns, and they had no time to take them up. One sailor and the captain ran along the beach; we cut down the three who stayed, though one sailor seized a boat-stretcher and fought hard. Presently Utumate and Tavu came back, saying that the captain had turned on Utumate with his fists, on which he ran back, and the sailor had escaped from Tavu by running into the thick bush, where we dared not follow. Then we cut off the heads of the three men we had killed." The sailor who escaped into the bush was the only survivor of this party. His name was Savage, and when it became dark he took to the water to swim three miles in the hope of finding some friend on shore. After a while some natives saw him, and came out in their canoes. As they approached, the poor fellow naturally gave himself up for lost. But when they were close to him a cloud covered the face of the moon, and the pursuers being either afraid or superstitious, turned back. When almost spent he touched on a sand bank, and at length reached the shore, where he fell in with Peter, a returned labourer, who took him to a chief named Tambukoro, who at this time was at war with Kalekona. By Peter's influence Savage's life was saved, and I met on my visit to this place Tambukoro and Peter (now our teacher there), and Vuria also. Poor Bower had an unfortunte fate. In place of taking to the water, he tried all night long to launch the boat; the marks of his feet were seen all round deeply indented in the sand. Then, when morning came, he climbed up into a big banian tree, where he was discovered by the natives and shot with one of his own rifles. His skull was found at Kalekona's village afterwards, recognized by the gold stopping in the teeth, and was reverently buried. Of course steps were taken to catch the murderers, and this was effected at last, and they were taken to the banian tree where Bower was killed, tied to it with ropes (which still hang there) and shot. Vuria was very young at the time, and was pardoned. Indeed it is doubtful whether any of the men would ever have been taken if Kalekona's son had not been promised his life on condition the others were given up.

Bishop Selwyn, the younger, was at Florida when all this trouble arose, and obtained such an influence over the people at this time that the work of the Mission took a deep hold. In 1884 six hundred were baptized in Florida, and in the last six years two thousand eight hundred have been added to the Church. What the mission now needs is a larger staff here to bring these Christians to Confirmation, and to build up their spiritual life. There is one deacon in Florida, Reuben Bula, a good man, though he does not possess the strong personality of Charles Sapibuana. I shall not easily forget Reuben; after a Confirmation at Mehaga, not far from Mboli, he presented me with a splendid crocodile's head in memory of my visit. A dusky crowd watched us as Reuben and Comins and I stood in the garden about the church. All around there was a sense of colour so rich and so dominated by scarlet hues that one felt conscious of a truly tropical experience. It was a garden of crotons, each plant ablaze with leaves of scarlet and yellow and purple.

The next morning the ship steamed through the Scudamore Channel and anchored off Mr. Neilson's store, and on the 21st of September we were at Honggo to assist at a function unique in my experience. We were close also to the home of Kalekona, and within a mile or two of Mandoliana. Early next morning we were at the beautiful church which now stands close to the spot from which Bower's murderers started; the photograph of this edifice is one of the best we took. Meanwhile canoes had been arriving laden with natives from all parts of Florida, no longer bent on bloodshed, but coming as delegates to the annual parliament, which this year was to be held at Honggo, whilst for weeks before the women had been preparing the great feast for these members of parliament. The teachers, of course, were there in force, besides many a chief known in days gone by as great warriors but now at peace with each other. At seven a.m. there was a celebration of the Holy Communion, and we administered to some forty of the delegates. At ten a.m. morning prayer was said in a crowded church and then the great function commenced. Let us imagine the scene. Under the shade of cocoanut palms and bananas, the sunlight throwing chequered shadows over the hard-beaten earth, there clustered rows of natives; the chiefs, with Tambukoro at their head, sat upon a form, looking most inelegant in European clothing. Their lowlier companions, clad chiefly in brown skin—and much more attractive in consequence—sat on the ground. In front of a bamboo house a kitchen table was placed, and I believe there was even a table-cloth. Behind it in the place of honour, as speaker and chairman, sat Palmer, looking wise and venerable with his white beard. Next to him I was placed, and the other clergy sat close by. Then up rose Palmer and opened the session. I had to follow: and as

Parliament at Hongso (Florida).

I uttered what in my opinion was a remarkably wise and judicious and eloquent oration, I noticed that Welchman was photographing us from a distance. I shall be eternally grateful to him for this act, because he happened to get into the foreground of his picture the beautiful back of a member of parliament, devoid of garments and most symmetrical in shape. I fear my splendid speech had little effect on the parliament of Florida, for as each flowing sentence emerged from my lips it was passed through the language of Mota by Palmer, who handed it on to a nervous teacher to be set into the Florida tongue for the ears of the assembled company; and I had the mortification of listening to my rounded periods reduced to two or three words in the third language through which it passed. Surely no premier ever fared so hardly.

One question that was then discussed reveals the difficulty caused by the transition from heathen to Christian customs.

A baptized Christian had married some near relative of his, and one who was upon the same side of the house as himself. (My readers will remember that in these islands the prohibited degrees are created by the existence of two sides of the house. A man may only marry some one on the other side of the house.) Now the natives would formerly have killed this man at once. What were they to do under present circumstances? Was it right to execute him now that they were Christians? Both the offenders had of themselves retired from Christian privileges, but it was still a grave offence in the eyes of the community. The parliament was clearly puzzled; so indeed was I. Towards the end of the day I heard that a teacher had made a capital suggestion. "Let us send the man to Queensland in a labour vessel."

And then it occurred to me how convenient such a place of banishment could become. The laws of Florida under the new *régime* are only three in number at present. The two first have to do with breaches of the seventh commandment: the third and last concerns the trespassing of pigs. And this is the law: If a pig is discovered on another man's land, the outraged landholder can shoot the intruder, but he may not touch the body. That can be carried away by the owner. The pig is of course a distinct feature of these islands—he is the chief treasure, and intrudes everywhere, and the doors of the churches are made high above the ground in order to prevent these quadrupeds from attending public worship. But to return to our parliament. I think the session for the year lasted but three hours. Happy Florida! Then came the distribution of food for the evening feast. Piles of flesh and yams and of other delicacies were heaped up in so many divisions; then each village bore away its portion in triumph. As soon as the parliament was prorogued, we entered the church once more and I confirmed some thirty-five persons, many of whom were delegates from their villages, who, as evening came on, all departed in their canoes. There had been no ill-will, no signs of hostility, and no one could fail to be struck with the change that had passed over this people in some fifteen years.

It would be impossible to tell the history of Florida without relating the result of the efforts of one of the earliest of the clergy in these parts in the matter of translation. He had not mastered the language, but yet he burned to be the first to give his people their Prayer-book in their own tongue. Now the hundred and fourth Psalm is one which is very early chosen for translation, and all went well till they came to the sentence: "Where the wild asses quench their thirst."

Nowadays the names of animals unknown to the natives are kept just as they are in English. And the stranger is surprised to see "sheep," "lamb," in the native Prayer-book. But the gentleman of whom I speak was bold. He produced the picture of a donkey, and asked his native teachers whether they had ever seen that creature. "Certainly," they answered. "There are animals just like that far back in the bush." Delighted beyond measure at having discovered so interesting a fact in natural history, he put down the native name given him. I may say at once that it denoted a mythical sort of pig. The next problem to solve was a native word for "wild." After attempting to explain, the teachers gave him a word which they said was often used to denote the qualities of the monster in the bush. The adjective really signified "man-eating." Now there was but one step more to be taken, "Quench their thirst." The clergyman explained that he needed something more than merely "drink." It must be a word expressing the drinking of some one very thirsty. The natives assured him they had just such a word as he wished for. And with delight the translator reflected that now he had done a good bit of work which would earn him the praise of the Mission. The word given to him had certainly a peculiar meaning. It denoted the manner in which a man drinks when he has the hiccups and is trying to check them! It will be enough to say that for months, and possibly years, the catechumens of Florida used to sing in the hundred and fourth psalm this startling paraphrase, "Where the wild man-eating pigs drink to stop the hiccups." The picture of a row of pigs suffering from hiccups is delightful. Every now and then in the old journals one comes across also a good answer to a question. The following is, I think, worth recording as the answer of a Florida man: "What is a lie?" "Gammon." Perhaps the following story will enable some to realize that a native may see no joke in what to one of us is extremely amusing. One of the clergy, I think Mr. Penny, had translated "The Tale of a Tub" for these people in order to amuse them. But they read of the tub and bunghole and tiger's tail and all, with perfect gravity, seeing no fun in it. But Mr. Penny was equal to the occasion. He remembered that the Florida man is by nature a shrewd man of business and keen at a bargain. He therefore ventured upon addition to the old story, ending it in some such form as this, "as the men had hold of the tiger's tail through the bunghole a man came along the road; they shouted to him to come to their assistance; but he stopped and asked, "What will you give me if I help you?" This was received with shouts of genuine laughter by the class; now at last they saw the joke! I cannot conclude this account of Florida, however, without giving two more extracts from Mr. Penny's book. The first illustrates the wise policy of the Mission towards native amusements.

"Dancing parties are among the most harmless of the native customs, and latterly we have been able to utilize them for the spread of Christianity. At first the Christians held aloof because of the Tindalo (ghost or spirit) influence upon the dancers, and because they would have to give up school and prayers during the tour. But when their numbers came to be considerable, the idea occurred to some of us to let a Christian party go attended by a teacher as chaplain, if the chief would consent to forego the Tindalo part of the business. On several occasions this has been done. A large dancing party started three years ago from Gaeta with a contingent of fifty Christians, and went the round of the Floridas. Each night and morning those men met together for prayers, and though at first they had to encounter ridicule, the ridicule in time gave way before their pertinacity."

The last extract has to do with the marriage question. "Bishop Selwyn makes it a *sine quâ non* that a polygamist shall put away all but one wife before he receives baptism. That this is the right course in Melanesia I cannot for a moment doubt, though the case of the woman put away is in some respects a hard one. . . . But she need not be homeless or friendless, or compelled to lead such a life as many of those who take the opposite view of this question assume to be inevitable. There are respectable people who will give her a home for the sake of her work, and with such she can live. Many of these women become Christians, and in the spiritual consolation and freedom from superstitious fear which they then enjoy, find greater happiness than they ever had as heathens; and though in their new life there may be somewhat of the hardness which Christianity accepts, yet they would not return to the old conditions so contrary to the faith in which they now find peace. . . . There remains the significant fact that in these particular islands a strong feeling exists in the minds of the native converts themselves against allowing a polygamist to receive baptism: and I feel sure that if an exception were once made, no matter how hard the case might appear at the time, it would set up a precedent most difficult to deal with in the time to come."

The happiness of the Christian life after renouncing heathenism is one of the bright joys of the work. Mr. Penny says, "We heard some men disputing about the 'new teaching,' and one said, 'While I believed in Tindalos I was like a woman carrying a load—I had to look where I trod, and I moved slowly; now I go where I like, and I am as light as a dead leaf.'"

At the same time there are special difficulties which occur when the new teaching confronts the old belief, and one of these deserves an allusion, it cannot be more. Before the introduction of Christianity there were found in every village women who were given over to an immoral life, but the faithfulness of the married women to their husbands was general. Now that the class of profligates has been made to disappear there are signs of the advent here and there of the same sin in a new form invading the homes of the married natives. But I must say farewell to Florida! loveliest of islands!

In 1895 a new central school was built at Siota on Mboli harbour. It is an experiment in order to utilize Norfolk Island more and more as a sort of university. It is hoped that boys and girls in the Solomons may first be taken to Siota, where there will be a permanent staff of the clergy, and for the first time women's work in the islands will be begun. The clergy of the Mission voted for this new enterprise in an island very far removed from Norfolk Island, on condition that if it proved successful each of the groups should in turn obtain its central school. It is obvious that this is a great forward move. One of its indirect effects may be that soon none of the groups will ever be left without a white clergyman. The schools are multiplying so fast that it will soon become impossible to give requisite teaching unless the staff is doubled and the higher teaching proceeded with throughout the year.

CHAPTER XX.

YSABEL (SOLOMON ISLANDS).

ELEVEN schools ; twelve hundred baptized ; two hundred scholars ; fifteen hundred listeners.

Ysabel is a large island not far short of a hundred miles in length. It has been already mentioned that here the Spaniards first landed in 1567, at a point about the middle of the north shore. And in this spot they built a brigantine, in which they cruised about the shores of this and of neighbouring islands. These early discoverers, though they came, in part, at least, for the purpose of converting the natives, seem to have been constantly in collision with them ; and the present history of Ysabel is also a very sad one. Cannibalism has been referred to as existing throughout Cristoval and Malcita, and many parts of Guadalcanar, but Ysabel has the unenviable distinction of being a hunting-ground for powerful tribes. In New Georgia there is a race inhabiting the Rubiana lagoons, which has infested the shores of Ysabel in order to get, by fair means or foul, as many lives as possible. They are, perhaps, the worst of all cannibals, and great is the dread in which they are held by all who live in these waters, whilst the effect of their raids has been, that of the hundred miles of Ysabel, eighty are practically uninhabited. The people have either been wiped out and eaten, or else they have migrated to safer quarters; and the only part which has an adequate population is the eastern corner. Here, for twenty miles or so, the villages are numerous. Some two thousand people inhabit them; and our Mission has taken a firm hold. Indeed, the day is not distant when they will all be Christians.

A distance of only twenty-five miles divides Ysabel from Florida, and to all appearance they are both full of harbours; and this some day will give them a great advantage over islands which cannot be approached without risk. As is usual in the Solomons, running streams are common. They empty themselves into bays, where the deposit they bring down creates mud-banks, and here the mangroves flourish, suggesting fever for the unwary. Mangrove swamps represent to those who have never seen them nothing but pestilential mud, full of crawling creatures among a hideous tangle of roots, covered usually with slime. Such a description is often true, especially at low tide, and when the traveller is actually threading one of the lanes which intersect these marshes. But it must also be remembered that there is in reality no more vivid and tender green than that of the mangrove. Seen, for instance, in the Scudamore Channel, in Florida, or in the harbour at Pahua, in Ysabel, these trees might be taken for masses of well-grown laurel or rhododendron planted round an ornamental sheet of water. In these harbours and along the coast there are a good many villages, many having moved down in order to be in Soga's country. But there are many gaps where natives used to live. Dr. Welchman, now in charge of the Mission, was asking one day, as he was sailing in his whaleboat along these shores, how this and that village had been destroyed; and he discovered that in about three out of every five cases the people had been wiped out by this same chief, whose protection is now sought by so many. A chain of hills acts as a backbone, and runs all down the whole length of Ysabel. But in some places the island is very narrow. I am not likely to forget the walk I had one hot and cloudless day from Pahua, on the northern side, to Perihandi, on the southern shore. It was but a few miles, but a hill of a thousand feet had to be climbed. The heat was tremendous, necessitating, for comfort's sake, at least, repeated halts; and the boys who carried bamboos full of water were often called to our side. From the summit of the hill a glorious prospect met our eyes; the shores extending right and left for miles, the *Southern Cross* anchored in a still harbour at our feet, and St. George's Island beyond, a fertile place, but totally uninhabited, because the fear of the Rubiana headhunters is still strong upon the people.

It was, I think, from the very hill upon which we stood, that, some years ago, a native rushed down to Bishop John Selwyn, who was lying ill of fever a thousand feet below, and begged him to come up at once, because "piccaninny" was dying. "Come quick." The poor bishop got up, and, medicine-chest on back, toiled up this ascent, a fearful tramp for a man in fever. When he at length reached the hut, the man showed him in the corner a litter of puppies, one of which was indisposed!

None of us who were of our company that day

are likely to forget the bathe in a cool stream when our journey was at an end. There was not sufficient depth for a swim; but we lay content and cool, each in a pool to ourselves. It is in Ysabel that the natives used, a few years ago, the tree-houses which have often excited the interest of travellers. They were meant as shelters when the raiders were signalled as approaching; but the introduction of firearms destroyed at once these strange places of refuge. In 1866 Bishop Patteson climbed up to one of these houses. Usually a tree with a straight stem is chosen, generally a banian tree. In one case the tree grew on the edge of a cliff, and the house actually overhung the abyss below. A ladder led up to it, and one of these was ninety-four feet in length, swinging in the air, with cross-pieces of wood loosely tied, and at very unequal distances. The ascent was of such a nature that even so experienced a sailor as Captain Bongard, of the *Southern Cross*, was fatigued when he reached the summit, and confessed himself relieved when he found himself once more on *terra firma*. The house itself was eighteen feet in breadth and eight feet high, built among the branches. The natives themselves seem perfectly at ease in such places, and do not know what giddiness means. Nor is this extraordinary when one of their daily duties is the ascent of cocoanut palms in order to get the nuts. A woman was seen ascending one of these ladders once with a load on her head, and not even using her hands. Another was walking about upon the branches at the height of a hundred feet, spreading out clothes to dry, perfectly unconscious of the results of a slip upon her part. Stones were piled up aloft as missiles for the heads of any who dared the ascent for a hostile purpose. But, as I have said, the houses have now disappeared, and at the present day the villagers choose the summit of a crag, and build up any parts which require artificial protection. I spent an afternoon in such a fort, and sat on a little bamboo verandah outside Dr. Welchman's house. On two sides were valleys of great depth, with their sides shrouded in the densest vegetation; birds were calling to each other, and white cockatoos sailed from side to side. Below us peeped out here and there the roofs of the village, built near the place of refuge. Ysabel differs from some of the islands further east in the fact that the chief is vested with great and really autocratic power. Soga, upon being asked what limits were put to his power, simply answered, "I speak and they do." It will be easily understood, then, how important it must be to the Mission to win the chief to their side. The history of our work here is briefly this: A visit of Bishop Patteson is recorded in 1862. As soon as the ship anchored at Sepi, the chief, Bera, came on board with a white cockatoo on his wrist, which he presented to the bishop as a token of goodwill. Four years later, the bishop remarks that though the people of two neighbouring villages were at war, still the opponents were willing to meet amicably on the deck of the *Southern Cross*. Meanwhile, in 1863, some boys were taken to Kohimarama, and were afterwards transplanted to Norfolk Island, but in the epidemic of typhoid fever in 1867 several of them died. In 1871 the Rev. M. Wadrokal was placed here, and the first school was opened at Mahaga, close to the harbour of Perihandi. In 1884, Bera, the chief, who had hitherto been an obstacle to the work, died. On his deathbed, he said, "Let no one be killed for me. Do no damage to the people's food or property when I am dead because of me. There has been enough of this. I did this when I succeeded to power; I have done so often. Soga and Soge must succeed me. I charge them to see these commands carried out." Accordingly, in place of killing victims at the dead chief's grave, Soga on this occasion took Bera's body and buried it secretly in the bush. But Soga was not yet a Christian. By his stronger personality he soon became the undisputed chief of Bugotu, and inherited the whole of Bera's power. His head-hunting continued, and he was the cause of numberless expeditions to wipe out neighbouring villages. But a change was soon to come over him and his people. In 1889 Soga was baptized; and ever since he has been the greatest possible assistance to the Mission. I have already stated that I have met three men who looked chiefs and filled their office well. Two of them are heathens: Natei of Santa Cruz, and Taki of Wango, in Cristoval. The third is Soga. He is not a great warrior in the same sense that the other two are, but he is a born ruler and a thoughtful man. And it is likely that his administration of justice will form an epoch in the annals of Bugotu. In 1890 he went to Gao, one of his villages. Upon his approach all the natives fled into the bush, remembering his old ways. But Soga called out, "Where are your chief men? Tell them to come to me. I have come in peace, and will do them no harm. Take my hand; there is no weapon in it. Of old I came here to fight, but now you need fear me no longer; that is all done with, for I am a Christian now." When the chief men at length appeared, he said to them, "You must sit down, and I will tell you what Christianity has done for Bugotu."

Let me now try and show by a few examples how Soga, at the present time, governs his people. It will be seen at the same time what delicate questions arise, and how hard it is to decide how far it is right to call in the power of the chief to enforce decisions. Let it be understood that Soga's people, numbering some two thousand, are all rapidly becoming Christians. Infanticide is not practised; indeed, the children are treated with the greatest care. A short time before I paid my visit a child died at Bugotu, and Soga fined the father because he considered that sufficient care had not been given to the child. Again, Dr. Welchman considered not long ago that the time had come to abolish the heathen custom connected with the marriage of widows. If a widow marries again in Bugotu there are customs which no Christian woman could submit to, and these could, up to the present, only be escaped by paying a fine; the consequence was that Christian widows did not marry again. Now, Soga could have abolished the old custom by his own authority. But was this the right method? Finally, the old law was declared to be done away with, and widows were declared eligible for re-marriage without penalties Soga then gave his consent to the new ordinance. But the feeling was very strong among the Christians. A great many did not come to prayers for a month, but the day was won; and almost immediately afterwards four widows were sought in marriage.

Here is another example. The heathen custom with regard to mourning was that the mourner should wear no ornaments, indulge very sparingly in washing, and attend no prayers in the church for the space of twelve months. Soga said the custom required modification, and that he would alter it. But he was asked not to take the first step, or rather, to use influence, not force. The duration of mourning was limited to a month, but there was to be no abstention from the daily public prayers.

Some time ago a man in Soga's territory quarrelled with a neighbour, and wounded him with a spear. Soga heard of it, and ordered the offender to live in the bush for a year, and not to come near the salt water. The gardens are all in the bush, so that it is not a question of starvation, but of banishment. The man, of course, obeyed. But the penalty inflicted is a striking testimony to the growth of the Spirit of Christ in one who, a few weeks before, was a noted head-hunter.

Again, not long ago a man was charged with embezzlement. He denied it, but it was proved to be true. Soga sent for the man to receive judgment. The accused, being a Christian by profession, supposed that he would not now be injured if he refused to present himself before the chief, therefore he did not come. Soga consulted Dr. Welchman on his course of action, and Welchman said it was a matter for the civil power, and the chief must punish for contempt of court. "Well," said Soga, "I ought to burn his house down, but," he added, "I don't like doing it. It brings my old heathen days back to me." Again he was told this was an act of justice, not of cruelty. One morning, therefore, forty men sat down by the offender's house before daylight, seized the culprit, took out of the house all that belonged to his mother, and then they burnt the house and all the property in it. After this they adjourned to the man's garden and destroyed that as well. This was for contempt of court; the penalty for the crime still remains to be adjudged. When it is remembered that there is no law here, except the power of the chief, it will be seen how wise was Soga's adviser, and how careful a missionary's conduct must be.

Turning now to the general habits of the people, it was a surprise to me to note the cleanly ways of the people. For instance, there are regular bathing-places set apart for men and women, and these are systematically used every day. Nor is anything like improper behaviour ever noticed. Their weapons for fighting are spears, but firearms are superseding them; and as Ysabel is under the German protectorate, it may be easy to obtain rifles. It is doubtful how far the Bugotu people have been cannibals; some villages have been given to this habit, but I believe Soga himself has never tasted human flesh. Let me now describe a Sunday I spent at Sepi, in Bugotu. At seven a.m. we had a celebration of Holy Communion. At ten a.m. Sunday school assembled; and as there were far too many for the church, the classes were scattered through the various houses. I inspected them all, first entering Soga's house, where I found the chief with some women in his room, to whom he was imparting instruction from the Gospels. And this was the man who five years ago was a head-hunting savage! In all I inspected eight classes, and counted about two hundred and twenty people, from grey-haired men to little children. The church was occupied by a class of nearly sixty adults, who were to be baptized in the afternoon. School was followed by morning prayer without an address. At all these church services I was made to sit in Soga's special seat; and here I will give an instance of the nice manners of the natives. No rule has ever been laid down that they are not to bring pipes into the church; but the natives have no pockets, and a man or woman carries a pipe in the ear or through one of the links of a necklace at the back of the neck. (I once saw in Ysabel a little girl of six with a black clay pipe stuck in her waist cloth.) The natives came to the conclusion that it would not be good manners to have these pipes in the church thus exposed; so of their own accord they placed a kerosene-tin case at the door of the church, pierced with countless holes. By the time service began this tin bristled with clay pipes, placed there by the worshippers. It was another fact of interest to note that stones were neatly placed in rows near the entrance of the church to make ornamental borders; and among these were embedded many tindalos, or magic stones. The old superstitions now lie at the door of the Christian Church, having lost their power.

By 2.30 on that eventful Sunday, September 18, 1892, a font had been erected in the open air under the shade of some young palm trees close to the beach; for, of course, the church was too small for the coming ceremony. Two large clam shells were firmly fixed on a structure, which was decorated with leaves and flowers, and in due time the service began, the whole population being assembled. Soga was there, and the catechumens stood in long rows near the font. I shall never forget the scene. A strong, warm sea breeze was blowing in our faces, bringing the waves up to the beach, but without violence, for a reef protects the shore. To our left, some two miles off, our floating home, the *Southern Cross*, was at anchor, the means whereby it has been possible to do so much for the Kingdom of Christ. Far away on the horizon were visible the blue masses of two islands, differing strangely at present in their spiritual history—

Florida, on the left, where the gospel has taken root so deeply; Guadalcanar on the right, to which our hearts turn with anxious desire, for, large as it is, our efforts have failed at present to get any hold over it. By the font stood Dr. Welchman. He it was who had dealt with these people, and his place it was to admit them into the ark of Christ's Church by the duly appointed way. To each candidate each of the four questions was put separately. Then one by one each came forward, and three times the baptismal water was poured. The shells were large—I suppose each half weighed forty pounds—yet they had to be filled three times (each time with the use of the appointed prayer) before the fifty-seven adults and six infants were all baptized. Thus ended one of the most striking services I have ever been privileged to take part in. Later in the day I asked for and obtained the shells. That evening, after the service was ended, we sat long in the twilight on the verandah of the clergyman's house, talking with Soga and his people about his early days. The air was still, except for the sound of waves at our feet upon the white strand, and the fireflies were twinkling and dancing in and out among the palm stems. The information we received from Soga I have placed under a separate head below. Let me give a few more details illustrating the chief's character. Dr. Welchman had been most anxious to finish the translation of the Gospels into Bugotu, and he asked Soga, the most capable of all his scholars, for his aid. Now, it must be remembered that persistent and sustained labours are not, as a rule, indulged in or appreciated by Melanesians, more especially when they are intellectual efforts. These last, indeed, are entirely new to the race, for, of course, reading and writing were unknown in

Melanesia till the advent of the missionaries. At first Soga was asked to come in the evenings. But his interest was so excited that he soon came of his own accord in the mornings as well, and often latterly he would suggest an afternoon sitting also, so anxious was he to complete the work before the *Southern Cross* should bear away the manuscript to Norfolk Island to the printing-press. Dr. Welchman called in teachers as well, but these one after another showed signs of weariness—and nothing was more natural—but Soga was always at his post, and nothing could damp his enthusiasm. So it happened that three times as much was effected as had been thought possible at first. The translation of the Gospel according to St. Luke formed part of these labours—indeed, this is usually the first Gospel given to the Christians, for obvious reasons—and when the 15th chapter had been completed, it was read over as a whole to Soga. The chief laughed loud and long. "It is good," he cried; "it is very good." Laughter is a sign among them of great pleasure, just as lifting the eyebrows is of an affirmative, and as silence is of thanks upon receiving a present. But I must bring the history of this island to a conclusion, though I would fain linger over it. I was ashore here for a longer period than anywhere else, and the work struck me as being peculiarly solid. It is worth mentioning here that when I asked the head native teacher at Sepi about the conduct of returned labourers, he told me that out of fourteen who had lately returned twelve were attending all Christian ministrations as before, and were only altered by the fact that they now understood a little English.

NEW GEORGIA.

No schools yet.

New Georgia has been known to the Mission chiefly as an island inhabited by bloodthirsty head-hunters and cannibals. The island of Ysabel has almost been depopulated by the people of Rubiana, which is part of New Georgia. But, in 1895, the efforts of some officers of H.M.S. *Penguin* have opened the way for the Mission. Lieutenant Somerville and some brother officers were camped on New Georgia, surveying the coast. They found the people in terrible dread of the white man, from experience of traders only. In a short time they learnt to look upon " man-o'-war men " as a different genus. This was a great step. The officers then discovered that some white men had filled the minds of the natives with horrible stories about " missionary men." The people said they had been told that " missionary men " would outrage their women, rob them of goods, etc. This is an instance of the difficulty of mission work where bad white men are first in the field. The reason for these calumnies is obvious. It does not suit dissolute men to spread Christian teaching. The officers nobly prepared the way for the Mission, and spared no pains to give the clergy all information. A chart of the anchorages has been supplied; the names of the villages and of the chiefs have been given; and, above all, a vocabulary of two thousand native names has been compiled for use, including several dialects. Such aid is a boon which cannot be too highly appreciated. Since then New Georgia has been circumnavigated by the *Southern Cross*. Probably 1896 will see the opening of a mission.

CHAPTER XXI.

THE NEW HEBRIDES.

THE Melanesian Mission now has charge of but three islands of this group—Raga, Opa, and Maewo. The Bishops Selwyn, the elder and the younger, ever willing to meet the wishes of other missionary bodies, gave up all the islands to the south and west of these—whether in the Loyalty Group, where a good deal of work had been done in the very early days, or in the New Hebrides—to the Presbyterian Mission, in order that a clear line of demarcation might be made. All, therefore, to the south and west of Raga, including the island of Espiritu Santo, is now in the charge of the Scotch Church. The reader is referred to the works of Dr. Paton and others for the history of these islands. There is some grand scenery in this group. The volcano of Tanna is well known. Ambrym is always covered with cloud and steam; Lopevi is another, and Merelava (in the Banks Islands) a cone descending abruptly into the sea.

Our three islands, then, are Raga, Opa, and Maewo, and the Rev. A. Brittain has them at the present time for his district, the Rev. C. Bice, who had worked for twenty-five years in the Mission, having given up the charge of the last two in 1891.

RAGA, OR PENTECOST.

Sixteen schools; six hundred scholars.

The English name originated in the name Isle de Pentecote given to the island by its discoverer Bougainville.

Raga has always been a difficult island for the missionary. Traders have known it for years; men-of-war have bombarded it; Frenchmen, as well as Englishmen, have helped to corrupt the natives. It is with a sigh that I think of a South Sea island which has been made almost impossible for Christian work by this kind of contact. Raga is our southernmost island, and I am not likely to forget my first Sunday in Melanesia, anchored at Steep Cliff Bay on the western shore, nor the strange foliage to become so familiar afterwards, nor the half-clothed natives and the coral beach. The mission history of this island is briefly as follows:—Before 1860 Bishop Selwyn picked up a lad who had drifted out to sea, and brought him back to his home in Raga. This boy, named Taroda, was attracted by Patteson in 1862, and came with him to New Zealand. Patteson mentions that he took away his poisoned arrows, to which he was much attached, and kept them for him. The old men in different villages along the coast have recollections of Bishop Patteson His height seems to have struck them. At one place a tree was carefully preserved until three or four years back, on which had been marked his height as he stood under it.

Year after year the *Southern Cross* touched here two or three times a year with varying success. In 1878, by the way, they saw the meeting between a returned labourer and his mother. The mother embraced her son's legs with rapture, the lord of creation magnanimously submitting. But not much work was done here till the advent of a Mota teacher, who has ever borne an excellent character—Thomas Ulgau ; subsequently his friend Maslea came to help him, another tried and trusted Mota man from that home of missionaries. This was in the days when the Rev. C. Bice superintended these islands. The two Mota men made their example tell, and when the Rev. A. Brittain took charge of this district he found a large number of Christians in the schools, the work, be it remembered, of native Christians themselves. One of the first teachers of Raga is named Tariliu, and was baptized Louis, after the Bishop of Kaffraria; he still continues at his work, and has always borne a high character. In 1882 Brittain had in his books the names of a hundred villages ; he complained somewhat piteously that it was not possible to visit more than one a day, for the natives gave him so hearty a welcome, and it was necessary always to stay for the feast and then to carry much food away.

It is said that labour vessels have been known to sell poison to the natives to be used against enemies ; even the clergyman is accused at times of such practices, and nothing in the Melanesian mind is perhaps too bad as coming from a white man in some places. Certainly the problem of language and nationality is a complicated one in these regions. Pentecost is only some two miles from Aurora, and it is ninety from Mota ; yet Aurorans speak more like Mota than Pentecost. Strange, too, are the customs. It is said that when a man is initiated into a higher rank in his village, one of the rules is that he should not wash for a hundred days—a veritable specimen of the old world belief in the odour of sanctity.

The latest news of mission life in Pentecost is cheering. In 1894 the first confirmations were held here. In 1895 there were more than a hundred adult baptisms. Some villages have become dissatisfied with school churches, that is, with buildings where the associations connected with worship are blunted by other associations connected with teaching and business and the thousand details of mission life. At Ulgau's station, which rejoices in the portentous name of Apalagalaga, a church pure and simple has been erected alongside of the school. So, also, we hear that Louis Tariliu, in a mission spirit, and of his own accord, and in the absence of the white clergyman, leaves his own school in competent hands and migrates to the district where he was born, and is so earnest in his efforts, supported by his wife, that in seven months a hundred people were attending his ministrations; and the numbers included men and women from the highest to the lowest, and children also. So even in Raga, spoilt by white men's sins, the light shines brightly under the guidance of the Mission.

OPA, OR LEPERS' ISLAND.

Five schools; two hundred and eighty baptized.

If Raga is demoralized by traders' influences it is even worse with Opa. Of course Selwyn touched here year after year in the very early days, but I cannot record any definite incidents till 1865. In this year Patteson found the people very wild, and he nearly lost his life at the hands of an infuriated man, who attacked him because a relative had been carried off by a labour vessel. In 1871 Mr. Bice was put down here for a fortnight, and was probably the first white man who had ever dared to stay unarmed and alone. A naval officer whom I once met told me that he was present on his ship when Bice landed, and he can never forget his feeling of admiration for one who seemed to be going so cheerfully to certain death. A fortnight later they found him well, to their very great surprise. The people at that time were entirely unclothed, and were great cannibals. Once Bice walked up to a village and saw a few yards in front of him an oven prepared for food: a man rushed out and implored him to go back, for the oven had been prepared for his body. Most strange were some of the customs: one of the strangest is that which forbids the meeting of a brother with a sister after a certain age. Dr. Codrington says natives do not like mentioning names lightly, and a man when asked the name of another will turn to some bystander, who answers for him, though he may know it all the while. So, again, a man in this island may speak to his mother-in-law, and she to him, but they will not come near.

In Opa the first Mission station was at Walurigi, a place that has now been abandoned, owing to the excessive mortality among the natives and the deportation of so many to labour fields.

After Bice had been a fortnight in Opa, he was taken away by the ship, and some canoes paddled out to bid him farewell. Some were upset and a few people were drowned; this, of course, was put down by the relatives to Bice's account, and when he returned next year they were ready to kill him. But a boy ventured out to the *Southern*

A Chief of Opa, New Hebrides.

P. 258.

Cross and warned Bice not to land. This boy's name was Tatamaeto, afterwards baptized Frank. He was a clever lad, but his subsequent conduct was unsatisfactory, and his end a sad one.

In 1873 four were baptized, the first from Opa. Christians began to multiply, and I read that at one time they considered that under the new faith they were not permitted to defend themselves against an enemy, but this fatal error was promptly corrected.

Tavolavola is now the principal station, situated near a regular forest of cocoanut palms, telling of a trader's station. Those who have been in these regions will recollect the trader Mousou, a Frenchman of doubtful antecedents, though always kind to the Mission. He had to escape for his life in 1892, and did not return.

Here, in 1885, the schoolhouse was burnt down by an angry father, who did not wish his son to attend school. The incendiary was much frightened after the deed was done, and the people helped to rebuild the school. Then the boy was permitted to return; he was baptized, and is now one of the head teachers.

In the next year we hear of a boy named Huhu baptized Peter. On his death-bed Huhu's father commended his son and his daughter Lingi to Bice's care. The boy became his inseparable companion, and went of course to Norfolk Island. While there he felt the peace and freedom from native temptations it affords, and said as he left, "I feel as if I had been in a great harbour." He returned to Tavolavola and did wonders at the school after the death of a well-known Christian teacher, and an Opa man, Tariqatu. Finally, after years of Christian work, Peter went to rest at Norfolk Island; there he became consumptive, and after long suffering lay face to face with death, full of the brightest hope and strong faith. On the morning of his release he called his friends round him and urged them to cling to Christ, and then he placed himself in God's loving hands in the words of his dying Master, "Father, into Thy hands I commend my spirit."

I have mentioned Charles Tariqatu. He was an excellent teacher, and great was the blow to the Mission when Charles one day was accidentally shot. Of course the unfortunate perpetrator of the deed trembled for his own life as soon as Charles should die. But Tariqatu sent for the boy, and placing his hands on his head he absolved him publicly from all blame, forgave him, and saved the boy's life. Such simple stories show how even in an island corrupted by evil European influences the grace of God has turned hearts and changed lives. So true are St. John's words, "The light shineth in the darkness, and the darkness overcame it not."

I conclude with one trait of native character. It has been already pointed out how delicate the natives of these latitudes are. Like peaches ripened in a hot sun, the slightest shock seems to upset their balance and causes death. Mr. Bice tells me that on one occasion he was in his bamboo house in Opa, when a man walked in and sat down. Now, Bice knew that this man had recently murdered one of the Mission people; whereupon Bice stood up and fixed his eyes sternly upon the new-comer. The man got up and retired from the house, walking backwards for some fifteen yards, and then turned round and vanished. He went home and said to his people, "The man looked at me." And in three days he was dead.

MAEWO, OR AURORA.

Seven schools; four hundred and fifty baptized.

One feature of the island of Maewo is known to every trader and labour vessel. A stream of clear fresh water empties itself into the sea on the western side, fed by a waterfall on the hill above, or rather a series of waterfalls. Boats can be taken into this stream, and tanks and casks can thus be filled in a brief space of time. The *Southern Cross* waters here regularly twice on her voyage; and pleasant indeed it is to know that clothes can be washed, and bathing can be indulged in whilst the boats' crews, composed of our native Christians, are filling the canvas tanks in the ship's boats. It is the custom to make up two such crews from among the Melanesians on board, and to reward them royally afterwards with tobacco and articles which they love. The waterfall itself is well worth a visit. The path winds up amongst dense tropical foliage, passing a banian tree covering about ninety yards square of land. At length the thunder of the water arrests your attention, and you stand under rocks over which a river dashes down, forming magnificent cascades of varied character in three or four different places. One of these I must describe. We stood at the edge of a great slide of water, reminding me of that wonderful spot described in "Lorna Doone" as leading into the Doone Valley. The stream was racing down about six inches deep, and it seemed that at the angle at which the slide was set no human foot could keep its position on it. What was my astonishment to see one of our guides quietly step on to the slide, and commence ascending it with the greatest ease! Behind him there yawned a gulf, for the smooth, slanting rock ended in a precipice, over which the stream thundered into a great pool thirty feet below. I was assured that I could without danger walk here also. Accordingly I attempted it, and discovered to my amazement that the rock was quite rough, owing to some deposit brought down in the water; and it was impossible to slip, whilst the stream struck one's foot and leaped up to the wrist. The return journey was accomplished among gardens of what the natives call qater. It is a species of arum lily, and grows best in water, the natives being ingenious in the way in which they carry the water from garden to garden.

This island was as wild and cannibal as Opa. One of Mr. Bice's first experiences is worth recording. He obtained permission to collect the children into a school, but of course they were entirely unclothed, in common with the rest of the population. After awhile Bice induced them to accept some strips of calico in the way of clothing, and, nothing loth, the children put them on and went home after school. In a few minutes Bice heard an uproar, and presently the whole village appeared armed and in furious excitement, prepared to kill him on the spot. Fortunately he knew enough of the language to understand that they were saying, "He has 'tapued' all our children!" He discovered that on the calico which he had given the children there was a mark like a cross, and two cross gashes is the "tapu mark" in Maewo. Of course he at once took away the calico and made many apologies. In 1873 the first baptisms took place; and then Bice was able to teach a lesson which could not fail to have had a permanent effect. After baptizing each person, he marked them on the forehead with the mark of the cross, and turning to the people he told them that these persons were "tapued" from sin! I am told that work here for years was very unsatisfactory. Little progress was made till in 1878 Bishop Selwyn made a protracted stay here. The result was that in the northern part of the island there were large and flourishing schools. But the population of Maewo has decreased very much owing to the labour traffic, and the schools are not as large now.

Some incidents during Selwyn's visit will be of interest. One day he was in a village, unconscious that a short distance away a horrible tragedy was being enacted. A mother desired that she might be buried with the corpse of her dead daughter, and the natives placed the living and the dead in a sack and trampled the mother to death. Selwyn was sitting at the time within three hundred yards, and knew nothing of it. At his earnest entreaty they promised never to repeat this horrible practice.

In Maewo they use mats dried in smoke as money. Fires are always kept burning under the mats, tended by men, and the more smoky the mat the more valuable is the money. So far as I know this custom is unique.

It was at Maewo that Bishop John Selwyn heard of his father's death. He went on board a trader's ship named the *Chance*, and the captain said to him, "Who is that Bishop Selwyn who died in England the other day?" Most difficult was it, the bishop said, to tell the Gospel story. They knew nothing of a king like Herod, nor of cows or shepherds or sheep. What could be made of a stable? Was it to be a worse structure than their own frail bamboo huts?

In 1879 we are told that the *Southern Cross* landed a boy on the rocks at his own village. The boy sat on where he was, looking miserable, and neither speaking nor being spoken to. Mr. Comins tried to get some of the natives to take an interest in him, whereupon one of them said, "There sits his brother, and that is his father." It was simply not etiquette to speak.

Towards the north end of Aurora there are two places on different sides of the island. Tasmate means "lee side," and Tasmori "windward side." It is astonishing to hear that these two names occur in Madagascar, and are placed in like positions. This and other indications of the like sort, point to problems relating to the diffusion of races which are not yet fully solved. Perhaps the best known school in Maewo is Tanrig, situated near the waterfall.

I conclude this with an account of two events, one at Tasmate, the other at Tasmori. In 1893, at Tasmori, Mr. Brittain was preparing four men for baptism—the last of the heathen population, who, up to this, had remained unconverted. He asked one man whether our Lord was seen on earth nowadays. "Yes," he said. And then he explained that two women had gone into the church after dark for prayer. There was no lamp there, but over the Lord's Table they saw a bright shining light, which remained there while they prayed and knelt. The same appearance was mentioned as having occurred at another school. There can be no doubt at all events of the simple and real faith of these people.

The other event happened at Tasmate, and was of a very different character. In October, 1892, in returning from the usual voyage, we anchored at the waterfall. The teachers told Mr. Palmer that a cutter had been attacked, the white men killed, and the goods taken out, the ship itself being at that moment aground near Tasmate.

Mr. Palmer and the captain and a crew started at once to inspect. They found the cutter on the rocks; everything on board was in wild confusion, blood was on the mainmast, and it was clear there had been an outrage. We reported the matter at Vila, and subsequently we learnt that a Frenchman named Pasnin had been killed by the boys on board, who were working as the ship's crew, assisted by some labourers who were being taken home, the shore people having nothing whatever to do with it. Of course, in due time, men-of-war appeared at the village, and, the true facts of the case being unknown, recourse was had to the bombardment of a village. It is needless to say how distasteful such work is, to Englishmen at least. They feel that these poor natives have, as a rule, been brutally treated in the first place. They have no courts of justice, but abide by the primeval custom of killing some one as an act of vengeance. My own experience leads me to take the side of the native in the first instance, and to put the blame on the white man. I was told that the man murdered on this occasion had been an oppressor of the natives for years. Deep and loud are the cries which rise up into the ears of the Lord of Sabaoth from the inhabitants of countless islands of the Pacific. Thank God the day of reparation has dawned at last. The evil deeds of the past are being avenged in the way Christians avenge—by giving them light and truth and the gospel tidings at the cost of the lives of some of our noblest and best. We do not grudge our best sons to these islands, nor to any other Christian cause.

APPENDIX I.

State of the Melanesian Mission in 1895.

	Population.	Baptized.	Confirmed.	Under Instruction.	Schools.	Teachers.
Raga	4000	250	25	400	7	17
Opa	5000	300	12	400	4	11
Naewo	4000	500	50	750	8	24
Merelava	494	205	12	494	5	20
Merig	36	16	0	36	1	4
Mota	800	770	109	770	7	28
Motalava	1013	1013	233	1033	9	36
Vanua Lava	1100	351	90	568	8	32
St. Maria	2800	644	38	1067	12	36
Rowa	37	37	2	37	1	4
Ureparapara	400	153	18	188	2	8
Toga	400	1	0	0	0	0
Lo	230	100	45	230	2	3
Tigua	300	23	0	250	3	2
Ilio	300	0	0	0	0	0
St. Cruz	40,000	88	20	250	3	10
Reef Island	400	0	0	0	0	2
Ulaua	500	110	16	240	3	12
St. Cristoval	20,000	60	6	230	5	20
Ugi	300	0	0	0	0	0
Malata	30,000	78	5	240	3	16
Guadalcanar	30,000	0	0	0	0	0
Florida	4000	3000	350	3500	28	66
Ysabel Bueno Vista	4000	1200	80	1500	11	30
Savo	500	30	0	0	0	0
	150,610	8929	1111	12,183	122	381

Melanesian Mission Staff, 1895.

BISHOP.—The Right Rev. Cecil Wilson, M.A., Jesus College, Cambridge, consecrated St. Barnabas' Day, 1894.

CLERGY—
　The Ven. John Palmer, B.D., Archdeacon of South Melanesia, 1894 (joined Mission 1863).
　The Rev. Charles Bice, S.A.C., 1867, Organizing Secretary, Australia.
　The Rev. Arthur Brittain, S.A.C., 1881.
　　,, Chas. Wm. Browning, M.A., 1892.
　　,, Rich. Blundell Comins, L.T., Dunelm, 1877.
　　,, T. C. Cullwick, 1877.
　　,, Walter George Ivens, M.A., 1895.
　　,, Leonard P. Robin, Hertford College, Oxon, 1892.
　　,, Henry Welchman, M.R.C.S., England, 1892.
　　,, Percy Temple Williams, M.A., 1895.
　　,, Richard Paley Wilson, L.T.C., 1895.
　　,, Reuben Bula, 1891.
　　,, Hugo Gorovaka, 1894.
　　,, Alfred Lobu, 1883.
　　,, Clement Marau, 1890.
　　,, Robert Pantutun, 1872.
　　,, George Sarawia, deacon 1868, priest 1870.
　　,, Henry Tagalana, deacon 1872, priest 1883.
　　,, William Vaget, 1892.
　　,, Walter Woser, 1886.

LAY WORKERS, European—
　Mr. Edgar S. Buchanan, M.A., B.Sc., 1895.
　　,, A. E. C. Forrest, 1886.
　　,, John William Williams, M.B., M.R.C.S., 1895.

LAY WORKERS, Native—
　Three hundred and eighty-one native teachers, besides two hundred in training at Norfolk Island.

APPENDIX II.

The Labour Traffic.

All are, of course, aware that it would be difficult to exaggerate the horrors of the labour traffic in the old days. There was no supervision, and the class of "beachcomber" was plentiful. The lives of men like "Bally Hayes," and the stories of South Sea life by Louis Becke, reveal the lawless conditions of trader life, and of traffic in labourers. They lived in an atmosphere of drink and dissipation. All was fair that procured a cargo. Even the present conditions of life round most—not all—trader's establishments militate strongly against mission work, for grog, at least, is sure to be plentiful. But the increased attention given to all South Sea problems by Colonial Governments and sympathetic naval men has made outrages difficult. It may be possible to do underhand things, but, as a general rule, the eyes of the authorities are very wide open, and numbers of philanthropic persons are on the watch for scandals. Furthermore, probably the whole Pacific population understands the conditions of plantation life. As regards the English countries, the physical needs of the labourers are well supplied. It is when we come to deeper needs that our doubts arise. I have had reason to modify to some extent the views I have expressed about the benefit derived by the natives by a sojourn in our plantations. That good arises in many instances there can be no doubt whatever. I have given already my own experiences in Fiji. In our New Guinea Mission, our native teachers, men of deep spirituality, are from Mollicolo and Tauna—two islands which are very difficult to touch. We know also of Guadalcanar men, who have gained "the best thing in the world" in Queensland, whilst we have no school in that island. On the other hand, it is probably true that thousands get no spiritual good in the plantations, but deteriorate. There is no conscious intention to injure them, but "no man cared for their souls." There is most earnest work being done in some places, such as Bwdobey and Mackay. But there is no system in it yet. Thousands return with a knowledge of vices, and of little else. Bishop Selwyn once asked a returned labourer whether he knew what Christmas Day was. The answer was that it was a great day for races. That was all he knew, and it is the only practical knowledge of the day among thousands of white men. Bishop Cecil Wilson sailed round Guadalcanar in the *Southern Cross*, and everywhere was met by canoes full of natives, among whom many could talk English, and had been to Queensland. When asked whether they wanted a school, they shook their heads. Mr. Forrest speaks of the French labour traffic to Noumea as an unmitigated evil. And I fear New Caledonia is not famed for its Christian work among natives. When one considers how little the average Englishman cares for the spiritual state of his white servants, one can gauge pretty accurately what he does for members of the black race. Still, the fact remains that the labour traffic may become a great engine for good. Under a proper system, by which labourers were received by Christian workers as soon as they landed, were handed on to the clergy, and were watched and guided till their time had expired, it would be impossible to exaggerate the amount of blessing which would attend such a scheme. To take a man away from savage surroundings, to place him among true Christians, and to restore him to his country again in three years, would be to make a missionary of him. And it is still true that natives who are most difficult to teach in their island homes have been transformed by Christian teaching in Queensland and Fiji. At the same time the clergy of the Mission complain bitterly of the depopulation of the islands by the traffic. A great many go away, and few return. The mass of those who return have learnt more about vice than about virtue. Certainly they have brought back some very terrible diseases. To sum up the question, it is necessary to say that, though it is a great opportunity, it is most often a cause of evil. But it is likely that, as the consciences of good people are touched, the efforts to benefit the natives will increase. We can but trust that if the traffic is permitted to exist, greater efforts will be made to remember that these people are guests of the English race, and have souls as well as bodies.

APPENDIX III.

Problems of the Future.

The questions discussed here have been talked over time after time with the clergy of the Mission. Some of the happiest hours of my life have been those spent on the *Southern Cross* when the day's work was done; and perhaps we were anchored near some coral shore, free to discourse about the work all loved so well.

The Central School.—As the Mission grows in force, corresponding changes may become necessary at Norfolk Island—simple developments to meet new needs. At present the number of the white clergy has been very small. The school for teachers has been taught by any of the clergy who happen to be at home. Of late, also, it has been the wish of the clergy to spend the whole summer in the islands, to get through necessary work. This tends to diminish the teaching staff at the central home. The question is now asked, whether the time has not come when there should be something like a distinction between various members of the staff. Some may be permanently located at St. Barnabas; others might be wholly sent into the out-field. It has been asked again whether the instruction at Norfolk Island would not be much more effective if it were carried on continuously by a permanent staff. Such changes foreshadow themselves as the number of teachers grows, and the strain on instructors increases.

The Island Staff.—Schools are multiplying so fast, and converts are so numerous, that it is considered doubtful whether the islands can in future be left without white supervision at any time of the year. There are so many to be instructed in the deeper teaching and prepared for Confirmation, that it is no longer possible to leave the groups without neglecting the work. It is asked how the extra help should best be given, whether by doubling the staff for two-thirds of the year, and leaving the islands alone for the usual months, or by supplying the place of one clergyman when he comes back by another. Both courses have their advantages. If two could work together they could more than double the effect. And it is still considered by some of the most thoughtful that there is great discipline for the native Church in leaving the native staff entirely alone for some months every year. It inculcates habits of independence. The stability of Christianity in the islands can be tested constantly by compelling the native Christians to think for themselves. The great danger in the South Seas is a weak leaning at all times upon the English staff. At the same time, it may well be that, as the islands are better known and are more frequented by white people, it may no longer be possible to leave Christian villages without some one who has authority with the alien races. The problem is an interesting one.

Central Schools in the different Groups.—The founding of a central school at Siota in Florida has already been alluded to. It is a momentous development, talked of for years, discussed by Bishop John Selwyn with his clergy, and at length attempted. It is still doubtful how the plan will succeed. It remains to be seen how the Melanesians will care to go to another island much like their own. One charm of Norfolk Island is the novelty of the surroundings. At the same time, it is much to be desired that the scheme may prosper. There seems a waste of power in taking natives from the Solomons and other groups to Norfolk Island on the chance that they will turn out well. Some of these importations show little stability of character, and return after a few months. All this might be prevented if some method of probation were employed at a school, such as Siota. Norfolk Island would then become a sort of university, with its trained staff, a school for the native clergy.

Women's Work in the Islands.—Women have never been sent into the islands. But as civilization progresses the time may now be ripe for such a development. Indeed, we are told that a married clergyman is to take charge of Siota, with his wife as an assistant. It is evident, of course, why women could not before be employed. The method of the mission has been to discourage a settlement of the white clergy in one spot, for fear that the natives should succumb to the influence of a superior race, obeying commands, but not with heart conviction. For this reason, the clergy hitherto have had no settled homes in the islands. Bamboo huts without furniture are provided for a temporary sojourn in the centres, and the whale-boat carries all the household goods. It is obvious that such a system precluded women's work. But the very methods employed have worked their true ends, and there are many places where women would be perfectly safe. Certainly at central schools this agency is urgently called for, nor can there be two opinions about the value of it. The influence of Christian women will work a revolution in the Solomons. Doubtless, it will have an effect also upon the floating white population.

Queensland and Fiji.—Can these centres of the labour traffic be made forces for the spread of the gospel? The day is past when the labourers were kidnapped. They go abroad now of their own free will. Surely it is the truest wisdom to accept the situation if the labourers are still to be recruited, and to turn what was once an occasion of falling into a means of grace. It requires a large outlay, and a man who will give himself to the work. Many mistakes will, doubtless, be made, but if a converging fire of Christian forces could be brought to bear on the islands, from Norfolk Island, from Queensland, and from Fiji, the result would be glorious.

Such are some of the problems which await the Mission staff, and they demand our sympathy, at least. It is believed that from time to time papers will be written by members of the Mission, setting forth questions which either press for settlement or call for investigation. Most of these are beyond the scope of a mere visitor to the Mission. For example, the *Mission ship of the future:* Will it possess sail-power with auxiliary screw, or will it be a steamer with auxiliary sails?

The Mission Language.—Will it always be Mota? Will central schools in the Solomons and Santa Cruz create more than one mission language? As the islands are opened up, what place will the English language take? How far is it possible to teach pure English alongside of the compound which is called Pigeon English?

Native Customs.—Now that we know more about them, will the Mission treat them as indulgently as in the past, or will there be a stronger effort made to supersede them? Lastly, and not least, as the Church in Melanesia becomes a settled Church, and thousands of children of Christian parents are baptized into it, how shall the indifference of universal Christianity be overcome? This evil must be faced, for history is full of the special dangers of the second stages of a Christian mission.

MAP
SHEWING THE PRESENT FIELD
OF THE
MELANESIAN MISSION

INDEX.

Amina, 199
Anaiteum, 4
Atkin, Joseph, 155-163
——, Mr., 5
Auckland, 3

Banks Islands, 44-87, 95-102
Baratu, Edmund, 60
Bauro, Michael, 171
Bice, Rev. C., 235, 236, 238, 242
Bower, Lieutenant, 211
Brittain, Rev. A. H., 12, 234
Bugotu, 225
Bula, Rev. Reuben, 213

Carlisle Bay, 145
Central School, 220, and Appendix III.
Codrington's Melanesian Folklore, 78, 88-93
Comins, Rev. R., 42, 171
Cullwick, Rev. T. C., 65

Espiritu Santo, 234

Fiji, 185
Florida, 203-220
Floyd, Rev., 186
Forrest, Mr., 133

Gaeta, 206
Gamal, 79
Gaua, 59, 60
Goodenough, Commodore, 146
Gorovaka, Rev. Hugo, 193
Graciosa Bay, 124

Guadalcanar, 189-197

Heuru, 173
Honggo, 214
Huhu, Peter, 239, 240

Jackson, Robert, 170
Johnson, 180
Jones, Rev., 186

Kalekona, 211
Kohimarama, 5
Koro, 59
Kulai, 85

Labour Traffic, 105, and Appendix II.
Lakona, 59
——, debtors at, 61
Lifu, 41
Loyalty Islands, 41

Mai, 42
Maewo, or Aurora, 241
Maleita, 175
Mana, 91
Marau, Rev. Clement, 68, 198, 200
Merelava, 66
Merig, 70
Monica, 137
Mota, 45
Motalava, 95

Natei, 134, 143
Nelua, 129, 133
New Georgia, 233
New Hebrides, 42, 234

Nobbs, 22
Norfolk Island, 1, 11-21
Norfolk Islanders, 22-27
Nukapu, 150

Olevuga, 206
Opa, 237

Padden, Captain, 4
Palmer, Venerable Archdeacon, 1, 12, 15, 113, 244
Pantutun, John, 13
——, Robert, 105, 112
Parliament, Native, 214
Patteson, 5, 41, 48-51, 150-159, 235, 237
Pek, 75, 76
Penny, Rev. A., 203
Pileni, 149
Port Adam, 180-184
Problems of the Future, Appendix III.

Qualges, 84
Qat, 99

Ra, 95
Raga, 235
Reef Islands, 148
Robin, Rev. L. P., 113, 115, 120
Rowa, 101
Ruddock, Rev. W., 193

Saa, 179
Sakelrau, Edwin, 75
——, Emma, 75
San Cristoval, 163
Santa Cruz, 123
Santa Maria, 58
Sapibuana, Rev. C., 208
Sarawia, Rev. G., 44, 47, 51, 52
Savo, 196
Sepi, 229, 232
Siota, 220
Soga, 226, 231, 232

Solomon Islands, 160
Southern Cross, Life on board, 28-35
Suqe, 78, 115
Suva, 186

Taape, 143
Tabular Statement, Appendix I.
Tagalana, Rev. Henry, 97
Taki, 169
Tamate, 63
Tambukoro, 212, 214
Tarigatu, 239, 240
Tariliu, Louis, 236, 237
Taroniara, Stephen, 155, 164, 167
Tasmate, 244
Tasmori, 244
Te Motu, 140
Torres Group of islands, 103
—— custom of honouring the dead, 111
Tughur, Ernest, 105

Ulaua, 197
Ulgau, Thomas, 236
Ureparapara, 82

Vaget, Rev. William, 19, 69
Vanua Lava, 74
Virsal, Benjamin, 77
Vureas, 77

Waaro, 200
Wadrokal, 131, 225
Walurigi, 238
Wate, Joseph, 179
Welchman, Rev. Dr., 104, 223, 227, 231
Wese, William, 199
Wogale, 103
Woser, Walter, 97
Wulenew, William, 105

Ysabel, 221

PUBLICATIONS

OF THE

Society for Promoting Christian Knowledge.

                                                                                                     s. d.

A Lady Born. By ELLA E. OVERTON. With Three page Illustrations. Crown 8vo...... ....*Cloth boards* 2 0

A Merry Heart. By H. MAY POYNTER. With Three page Illustrations. Crown 8vo. ....*Cloth boards* 1 6

Abbotsnid. By C. E. M., author of "Adam Gorlake's Will." With Four page Illustrations. Crown 8vo.......*Cloth boards* 3 0

Adventurous Voyage of the "Polly," and other Yarns. By the late S. W. SADLER, R.N. With Four page Illustrations. Crown 8vo. ....*Cloth boards* 2 6

All is Lost save Honour. A Story of To-day. By CATHERINE M. PHILLIMORE. With Three page Illustrations. Crown 8vo. ....*Cloth boards* 1 6

Alone among the Zulus. By a PLAIN WOMAN. The Narrative of a Journey through the Zulu Country. With Four page Illustrations. Crown 8vo. ....*Cloth boards* 1 6

Another Man's Burden. A Tale of Love and Duty. By AUSTIN CLARE. With Four page Illustrations. Crown 8vo....................... ....*Cloth boards* 3 6

An Idle Farthing. By ESMÈ STUART. With Three page Illustrations. Crown 8vo. ....*Cloth boards* 2 0

PUBLICATIONS OF THE SOCIETY

	s.	d.
Baron's Head (The). By FRANCES VYVIAN. With Three page Illustrations. Crown 8vo. ....*Cloth boards*	2	6
Belfry of St. Jude (The). A Story. By ESMÉ STUART, author of "Mimi." With Three page Illustrations. Crown 8vo. ....*Cloth boards*	2	6
Bernard Hamilton, Curate of Stowe. By MARY E. SHIPLEY, author of "True to Herself," etc. With Four page Illustrations. Crown 8vo. ....*Cloth boards*	3	0
Brotherhood; or, In the Way of Temptation. With Three page Illustrations. Crown 8vo............*Cloth boards*	1	6
By Lantern Light. A Tale of the Cornish Coast. By AUSTIN CLARE, author of "Another Man's Burden," etc. With Four page Illustrations. Crown 8vo........*Cloth boards*	3	6
Chryssie's Hero. By ANNETTE LYSTER, author of "Fan's Silken String." With Three page Illustrations. Crown 8vo. ....*Cloth boards*	2	6
Conroy Cousins (The). By the Rev. E. N. HOARE. With Four page Illustrations. Crown 8vo. ....*Cloth boards*	3	6
Dodo: an Ugly Little Boy; or, Handsome is that Handsome does. By E. EVERETT GREEN. With Three page Illustrations. Crown 8vo. ....*Cloth boards*	2	0
Engel the Fearless. By ELIZABETH H. MITCHELL. With Four page Illustrations. Crown 8vo............*Cloth boards*	3	6
Fairhope Venture (The). An Emigration Story. By the Rev. E. N. HOARE. With Four page Illustrations. Crown 8vo............*Cloth boards*	3	6
For Better for Worse. By CATHERINE E. SMITH. With Three page Illustrations. Crown 8vo. ....*Cloth boards*	2	0
George Brand, Cabinet-Maker. By Rev. E. L. CUTTS. With Three page Illustrations. Crown 8vo. ...*Cloth boards*	1	6
Hasselaers (The). A Tale of Courage and Endurance. By E. E. COOPER. With Three page Illustrations. Crown 8vo. ....*Cloth boards*	1	6
Here and Elsewhere. The Fortunes of George Adams, in Town and Country. By the Rev. HARRY JONES, M.A. Crown 8vo............*Cloth boards*	2	0

	s.	d.
How to Make Common Things. For Boys. By JOHN A. BOWER. Copiously Illustrated. Crown 8vo. *Cloth bds.*	3	6
Invasion of Ivylands (The). By ANNETTE LYSTER, author of "Fan's Silken String." With Three page Illustrations. Crown 8vo.............................*Cloth boards*	1	6
Jack's Little Girls. By ALICE F. JACKSON. With Four page Illustrations. Crown 8vo. ....*Cloth boards*	3	0
Jennifer's Fortune. By Mrs. HENRY CLARKE, M.A. With Four page Illustrations. Crown 8vo.......*Cloth boards*	3	6
Kate, the Pride of the Parish. By ELIZABETH H. MITCHELL. Three page Illustrations. Crown 8vo. *Cloth bds.*	2	6
Little Lady Maria. By the Author of "The Dean's Little Daughter." Four page Illustrations. Crown 8vo. ...*Cloth*	3	0
Mike. A Tale of the Great Irish Famine. By the Rev. E. N. HOARE, M.A. With Three page Illustrations. Crown 8vo..*Cloth boards*	1	6
Mrs. Dobbs' Dull Boy. By ANNETTE LYSTER, author of "Northwind and Sunshine," etc. With Three page Illustrations. Crown 8vo............................*Cloth boards*	2	6
Percy Trevor's Training. By the Rev. E. N. HOARE. With Three page Illustrations. Crown 8vo. ...*Cloth boards*	2	6
Perseverance under Difficulties, as shown in the Lives of Great Men. Illustrated. Crown 8vo. ......*Cloth boards*	2	0
Philip Vandeleur's Victory. By C. H. EDEN, author of "Australia's Heroes," etc. With Three page Illustrations. Crown 8vo. ....*Cloth boards*	2	0
Pillars of Success (The). By CRONA TEMPLE, author of "Griffinhoof," etc. With Three page Illustrations. Crown 8vo..*Cloth boards*	2	6
Prisoner of the Pampas (The); or, The Mysterious Seal Island. By CHARLES H. EDEN. With Three page Illustrations. Crown 8vo........................*Cloth boards*	2	6

PUBLICATIONS OF THE SOCIETY

	s.	d.
Remarkable Men: Wotton, Ferguson, Humboldt, Wilberforce, Faraday, Scott, Arnold, Waterton, Roberts, Bunyan. Illustrated. Crown 8vo. ....*Cloth boards*	2	0
Second Sight. By A. EUBULE-EVANS. With Three page Illustrations. Crown 8vo. ....*Cloth boards*	2	6
Simple Experiments for Science Teaching. By JOHN A. BOWER With numerous Woodcuts. Crown 8vo...............*Cloth boards*	2	6
Slavers and Cruisers. A Tale of the West Coast. By the late S. W. SADLER, R.N. With Four page Illustrations. Crown 8vo. ....*Cloth boards*	3	0
Squatter's Home (The). By MARIANNE FILLEUL, author of "Marion, or the Smuggler's Wife." With Three page Illustrations. Crown 8vo...............*Cloth boards*	2	0
Squire of Bratton (The). By the author of "The Dean's Little Daughter." With Three page Illustrations. Crown 8vo...............*Cloth boards*	2	0
Standard Bearers. A Story of Church Defence. By AUSTIN CLARE. With several Illustrations. Crown 8vo. *Cloth boards*	1	6
Stepmother's Will (The); or, a Tale of Two Brothers. By A. EUBULE-EVANS. With numerous Illustrations. Crown 8vo. ....*Cloth boards*	2	6
Stories of Success, as illustrated by the Lives of Humble Men who have made themselves Great. By JAMES F. COBB, Esq. With Three page Illustrations. Crown 8vo...............*Cloth boards*	2	6
Story of Our Museum (The): showing how we formed it, and what it taught us. By the Rev. H. HOUSMAN, B.D. With numerous Illustrations. Crown 8vo.......*Cloth boards*	2	6
Sweet William. By Mrs. THOMAS ERSKINE. With Three page Illustrations. Crown 8vo...............*Cloth boards*	1	6

FOR PROMOTING CHRISTIAN KNOWLEDGE.   5

	s.	d.
Three Martyrs of the Nineteenth Century. Studies from the Lives of Livingstone, Gordon, and Patteson. By Mrs. RUNDLE CHARLES. Crown 8vo. .... *Cloth boards*	3	6
"Through all the Changing Scenes of Life." By S. BARING-GOULD. With several Illustrations. Crown 8vo..*Cloth boards*	1	6
Through the Rough Wind. A Story of the Collieries. By CRONA TEMPLE. With Three page Illustrations. Crown 8vo..*Cloth boards*	1	6
Tre, Pol, and Pen. By F. FRANKFORT MOORE. With Three page Illustrations. Crown 8vo............*Cloth boards*	2	6
Twilight: A Story of Two Villages. By ANNETTE LYSTER. With Three page Illustrations. Crown 8vo. ...*Cloth boards*	2	6
Unsettled for Life; or, What shall I be? By the Rev. HARRY JONES, M.A. Crown 8vo ....*Cloth boards*	2	6
Velveteens. By the Rev. E. GILLIAT, M.A. With Three page Illustrations. Crown 8vo. ....*Cloth boards*	2	6
What came Between. By Mrs. NEWMAN. With Four page Illustrations. Crown 8vo......................*Cloth boards*	3	0

BY G. MANVILLE FENN.

Crown 8vo. With Five page Woodcuts. Cloth boards, 5s. each.

Crown and Sceptre: A West Country Story.

Gil the Gunner; or, The Youngest Officer in the East.

Mass' George; or, A Boy's Adventures in the Old Savannahs.

Sail Ho! or, A Boy at Sea.

The Vast Abyss.

To the West.

BY GORDON STABLES, M.D., C.M., R.N.

Crown 8vo. Illustrated. Cloth Boards.

Born to Command: A Tale of the Sea and of Sailors. 5*s.*
Captain Japp; or, The Strange Adventures of Willie Gordon. 5*s.*
Children of the Mountains. A Story of Life in Scottish Wilds. 5*s.*
"From Greenland's Icy Mountains." A Tale of the Polar Seas. 2*s.*
Harry Wilde: a Tale of the Brine and the Breeze. 3*s.*
In Touch with Nature: Tales and Sketches from the Life. 2*s.*
Rocked in the Cradle of the Deep: a Tale of the Salt, Salt, Sea. 2*s.* 6*d.*

BY F. FRANKFORT MOORE.

Crown 8vo. Illustrated. Cloth boards.

Coral and Cocoa-nut. The Cruise of the Yacht "Firefly" to Samoa. 3*s.* 6*d.*
Fireflies and Mosquitoes. 3*s.* 6*d.*
From the Bush to the Breakers. 3*s.* 6*d.*
Sailing and Sealing. A Tale of the North Pacific. 3*s.* 6*d*
The Fate of the "Black Swan." A Tale of New Guinea. 3*s.*
The Great Orion. 2*s.* 6*d.*
The Ice Prison. 3*s.*
The Mutiny on the "Albatross." 3*s.* 6*d.*
The Slaver of Zanzibar. 3*s.*
The Two Clippers. 3*s.* 6*d.*
Tre, Pol, and Pen. 2*s.* 6*d.*
Will's Voyages. 3*s.*

BY THE LATE W. H. G. KINGSTON.

Illustrated. Cloth boards.

Michael Penguyne; or, Fisher Life on the Cornish Coast. Crown 8vo, 1s. 6d.

Mountain Moggy; or, The Stoning of the Witch. Post 8vo, 1s.

Ned Garth; or, Made Prisoner in Africa. A Tale of the Slave Trade. Crown 8vo, 2s. 6d.

Owen Hartley; or, Ups and Downs. Crown 8vo, 2s. 6d.

Rob Nixon, the Old White Trapper. A Tale of Central British North America. Post 8vo, 1s.

Sunshine Bill. Crown 8vo, 1s. 6d.

The Cruise of the "Dainty." Crown 8vo, 1s. 6d.

The Frontier Fort; or, Stirring Times in the North-West Territory of British America. Crown 8vo, 1s. 6d.

The Gilpins and their Fortunes. A Tale of Australia. Crown 8vo, 1s. 6d.

The Lily of Leyden. Post 8vo, 1s.

The Log House by the Lake. A Tale of Canada. Post 8vo, 1s.

The Mate of the "Lily;" or, Notes from Harry Musgrave's Log-Book. Crown 8vo, 1s. 6d.

The Settlers. A Tale of Virginia. Crown 8vo, 2s. 6d.

The Two Shipmates. Crown 8vo, 1s. 6d.

The Two Whalers; or, Adventures in the Pacific. Post 8vo, 1s.

BY MRS. MOLESWORTH.

A Charge Fulfilled. With Three page Illustrations. Crown 8vo, cloth boards, 2s. 6d.

A House to Let. With Coloured Illustrations. Small 4to, cloth boards, 2s. 6d.

Family Troubles. With Coloured Illustrations. Small 4to, cloth boards, 1s.

Five Minutes' Stories. With Coloured Illustrations. Small 4to, cloth boards, 2s. 6d.

Great Uncle Hoot-Toot. With several Illustrations. Small 4to, cloth boards, 2s.

Lettice. With Three page Illustrations. Crown 8vo, cloth bds., 1s. 6d.

The Abbey by the Sea, and another Story. With One page Illustration. Post 8vo, cloth boards, 1s.

The Little Old Portrait. With One page Illustration. Post 8vo, cloth boards, 1s.

The Lucky Ducks, and other Tales. With Coloured Illustrations. Small 4to, cloth boards, 2s. 6d.

The Man with the Pan-Pipes, etc. With Coloured Illustrations. Small 4to, cloth boards, 2s. 6d.

The Thirteen Little Black Pigs, and other Stories. With Coloured Illustrations. Small 4to, cloth boards, 2s. 6d.

Twelve Tiny Tales. With Coloured Illustrations. Small 4to, cloth boards, 2s. 6d.

LONDON: NORTHUMBERLAND AVENUE, W.C.;
43, QUEEN VICTORIA STREET, E.C.

www.ingramcontent.com/pod-product-compliance
Lightning Source LLC
Chambersburg PA
CBHW030816230426
43667CB00008B/1235